THiNK

STUDENT'S BOOK 1

Herbert Puchta, Jeff Stranks & Peter Lewis-Jones

CAMBRIDGE
UNIVERSITY PRESS

CONTENTS

PRONUNCIATION	THINK	SKILLS	
Vowel sounds: /ʊ/ and /uː/	**Values:** Caring for people and the environment **Self esteem:** Classroom rules	Reading	Article: Just because I didn't want to take a bath Website: Product reviews Photostory: The treasure hunt
		Writing	A paragraph about housework
		Listening	Radio programme – advice for young inventors
Strong and weak forms of *was* and *were*	**Values:** Trying, winning and losing **Train to Think:** Sequencing	Reading	Article: If you don't give up, you can't fail Web forum: Your favourite sports fails! Culture: The Olympic Games – the good and the not-so-good
		Writing	An article about a sporting event
		Listening	Teens talking about sport

PRONUNCIATION	THINK	SKILLS	
Vowel sounds: /ɪ/ and /aɪ/	**Values:** Valuing our world **Self esteem:** Being brave is …	Reading	Article: An amazing place Article: Could you live there? Photostory: The competition
		Writing	An email about a place in the article
		Listening	Interview with a Kalahari bushman
Voiced /ð/ and unvoiced /θ/ consonants	**Values:** Appreciating other cultures **Train to Think:** Problem solving	Reading	Blogs: Alice's world, The life of Brian Letters to a newspaper: Our town: what's wrong and what can we do about it? Culture: Ghost towns around the world
		Writing	An informal email
		Listening	A conversation between people arranging to go out

PRONUNCIATION	THINK	SKILLS	
The /h/ consonant sound	**Values:** Exercise and health **Self esteem:** Getting help	Reading	Article: Changing bodies Webchats: Crazy things that parents say to their kids Photostory: The phone call
		Writing	A phone message
		Listening	Dialogues about physical problems
Sentence stress	**Values:** Travel broadens the mind **Train to Think:** Exploring differences	Reading	Blog: The non-stop traveller Interview: The taxi driver Culture: Hard journeys for schoolchildren
		Writing	An essay about someone you admire
		Listening	A traveller talking to children at his old school

7 | THE EASY LIFE

A

READING

1 🔊2.03 **What are the objects here? Match the words in the list with the photos. Write 1–6 in the boxes. Listen, check and repeat.**

1 e-reader | 2 digital camera | 3 flat screen TV
4 tablet | 5 laptop | 6 (desktop) computer

B

C

D

2 SPEAKING **Work in pairs. Talk about the objects with a partner.**

> I've got a …   I haven't got a …

> I think the (laptop) in the photo looks (cool / really new / quite old).

E

F

3 SPEAKING **Imagine you could only have one of these things. Which would you choose?**

> I'd choose the …
> It's important for me because …
> What about you?

4 🔊2.04 **Read the sentences and guess the correct answer. Listen and check your answers.**

1 A person who **invents** something *has got an idea and creates something new / has got enough money to buy something new.*

2 If you hear something that is **shocking** it makes you feel *happy and excited / surprised and upset.*

3 I **researched** the topic *on the camera / on the Internet.*

4 What is a **huge** problem for Africa? *There is not enough clean water / There is not enough space for people.*

5 You can get **trachoma** from *dirty water / bad food.*

6 Getting an **eye infection** can make people *deaf / blind.*

7 You buy **gel** in a *plastic bottle / paper bag.*

5 SPEAKING **Work in pairs. Look at the title of the article and the photos on the next page. What do you think the article is about? Compare your ideas with other students.**

6 🔊2.05 **Read and listen to the article about a young inventor. Are the sentences true (T) or false (F)? Correct the false ones.**

0 Ludwick Marishane is from South Africa. *T*

1 Ludwick used his laptop to find out more about the world's water situation.

2 Millions of people get trachoma every year.

3 Trachoma is an illness that makes people blind.

4 Ludwick wanted to help people with trachoma.

5 Ludwick's dream was to help people find clean water.

6 'DryBath' is helping to save a lot of water all over the world.

7 DryBath is a success.

8 Ludwick wants to invent more things.

'... just because I didn't want to take a bath'

LUDWICK MARISHANE, a 17-year-old South African, was with his friends in Limpopo when they started talking about inventing something to put on your skin so you don't have to take a bath. Ludwick thought that this was a great idea. He used his mobile to do some research on the Internet, and he found some shocking facts.

Two point five billion people around the world haven't got clean water. This is a huge problem because dirty water can create terrible illnesses. One of them is trachoma: eight million people all over the world get trachoma every year. They wash their faces with dirty water, get an infection and become blind. To stop trachoma, people don't have to take expensive medication. They don't have to take pills. They don't have to have injections. They have to wash their faces with clean water. That's it.

Ludwick started thinking. He wanted to make something to help people in parts of the world where it's difficult to find clean water. He did more research on his mobile, and he did more thinking. Ludwick had a plan. He wanted to make a gel for people to put on their skin so they don't have to take a bath. He wrote the formula for the gel on his mobile phone. When he was at university, he never stopped thinking about his invention. He started to talk to other people about it, and three years later the dream came true. He made the gel and called it 'DryBath'.

Ludwick Marishane is the winner of lots of prizes. People call him 'one of the brightest young men in the world'. He is very happy about his success. DryBath is helping people to be healthy. And DryBath also helps to save water. That's important in many parts of the world where it's difficult to find clean water. Now he wants to invent other things, and he wants to help other young people to become inventors too.

■ THiNK VALUES ■

Caring for people and the environment

1 **Match the values in the list with the sentences in the speech bubbles. Write a–d in the boxes.**

a caring about the environment
b caring about the quality of your work
c caring about your appearance
d caring about other people

1 *The water in a lot of rivers and lakes is not clean.* ☐

2 *I need to wash my hair. It's dirty.* ☐

3 *Are you feeling cold? I can give you my jumper.* ☐

4 *Can you switch off the radio, please? I'm doing my homework.* ☐

2 **SPEAKING** Work in pairs. Ask and answer questions about Ludwick Marishane. Try and find as many answers as possible.

Does he care about the environment? his appearance? the quality of his work? other people?

Yes, because DryBath helps to save water.

GRAMMAR
have to / don't have to

1 Complete the sentences from the article on page 67 with *have to* and *don't have to*.

1 They _____ wash their faces with clean water.
2 To stop trachoma people _____ take expensive medication.

2 Complete the rule and the table.

> **RULE:** Use ¹_____ to say 'this is necessary'.
> Use ²_____ to say 'this isn't necessary'.

Positive	Negative
I/you/we/they ⁰ *have to* help	I/you/we/they don't have to help
he/she/it ¹_____ help	he/she/it ²_____ help

Questions	Short answers
³_____ I/you/we/they have to help?	Yes, I/you/we/they do. No, I/you/we/they don't.
⁴_____ he/she/it have to help?	Yes, he/she/it ⁵_____ . No, he/she/it ⁶_____ .

3 Match the sentences with the pictures.

1 The bus leaves in 20 minutes. He has to hurry.
2 The bus leaves in 20 minutes. He doesn't have to hurry.

4 Complete the sentences with *have to / has to* or *don't / doesn't have to*.

1 Our teacher doesn't like mobile phones. We _____ switch them off during lessons.
2 I know that I _____ work hard for this test! You _____ tell me!
3 My sister is ill. She _____ stay in bed.
4 Your room is terrible! You _____ tidy it up.
5 Mario's English is perfect. He _____ study for the tests.
6 I can hear you very well. You _____ shout!

> Workbook page 64 ▶

VOCABULARY
Gadgets

1 ◀)2.06 Match the words with the photos. Write 1–10 in the boxes. Then listen, check and repeat.

1 satnav | 2 MP3 player | 3 torch | 4 games console |
5 remote control | 6 coffee machine | 7 calculator |
8 docking station | 9 hair dryer | 10 headphones |

2 How important are these gadgets for you? Make a list from 1 to 10 (1 = most important, 10 = not important at all).

3 SPEAKING Work in pairs. Compare your ideas and tell your partner how often you use these gadgets.

> I often use …
> I use my … almost every day.
> What about you?
> I rarely use …

> Workbook page 66 ▶

LISTENING

1 **SPEAKING** Look at the pictures of different inventions. Match them with the phrases. Write 1–4 in the boxes. Then make sentences to explain what the inventions are. Compare your ideas in class.

A

B

C

D

1 not tidy up room / have got robot
2 machine help / ride bike up a hill
3 invention help homework / more time for friends
4 machine can get places around the world / 10 seconds

> *The girl in picture A has got a cool machine. It helps her to ride her bike up a hill.*

2 **2.07** Martin and Anna want to become inventors. Try and match the sentence parts to find out what their situation is. Then listen and check.

1 Martin has got an idea for an invention,
2 He's got a job,
3 Anna has got a lot of ideas,
4 She's thirteen,

a and wants to be an inventor.
b but doesn't want to say what it is.
c but doesn't know where to start.
d and hasn't got enough time to work on it.

3 **2.07** Complete the expert's answers with *should* or *shouldn't*. Listen again and check.

1 You _____ start thinking 'What idea can I have to make a million pounds?'
2 You _____ start with a little idea.
3 You _____ think 'What can I invent that makes one little thing in my life easier'?
4 You _____ give up your job.
5 You _____ work on your best idea first.
6 You _____ forget about your other ideas.

GRAMMAR
should / shouldn't

1 Look at the sentences in Exercise 3 of the listening. Match the sentence parts in the rule.

> **RULE:**
> 1 Use *should* to say
> 2 Use *shouldn't* to say
> a 'It's not a good idea.'
> b 'It's a good idea.'

2 Use *should / shouldn't* and a word from each list to give advice to these people.

~~take~~ | go to | eat | drink | read
~~aspirin~~ | book any more | bed
any more cake | water

0 I've got a headache. *You should take an aspirin.*
1 I'm really thirsty. _____
2 My eyes are tired. _____
3 I'm tired. _____
4 I feel sick. _____

Workbook page 64 ➤

SPEAKING

Read the sentences. Decide whether you agree or disagree. Then work in pairs. Tell your partner.

1 Students shouldn't take phones into their lessons.
2 Students should use computers in all lessons.
3 There should only be six students in a classroom.
4 Students shouldn't wear school uniforms.

> *I disagree with number 2. Students should use computers in most subjects, but not in all of them. That would be boring.*

READING

1 SPEAKING **Work in pairs. Look at the pictures and think about what the machines do. Then choose one of the two machines and talk about it.**

> I think it's called ...   It helps with ...
> It's a cool machine because ...
>   It gets angry when ...

2 **Read these product reviews on a website from the year 2066. What do the robots do?**

I bought the Sunny Star robot two weeks ago. It does everything for me in the morning. I don't have to do anything. It wakes me up with a nice song. I don't have to get out of bed myself. It helps me to get out of bed and carries me to the shower. Then it washes my face and brushes my teeth. It makes my bed and packs my bags for school. But you should be careful! You mustn't use it on rainy days. Sunny Star gets very angry when it rains. Then it only turns the cold water on when it puts you in the shower!

Do you like visiting other countries? Yes?

Then this invention is perfect for you. You don't have to have a lot of money. And you don't have to get up in the morning. It looks like a bed. It's got a computer. You only have to type the name of a city, and it flies you there. You can stay in bed, and you can have breakfast too. But don't tell your teachers! They would take it away from you! Oh, and there's one more thing you should know. You mustn't forget to switch Travel Plus off at night. Do you know why? Because it wants to travel day and night. It waits until you're sleeping and then it starts travelling. Then you might wake up at the North Pole or in the middle of the ocean!

3 **Read the reviews again and answer the questions.**

1 What's the first thing that Sunny Star does for you in the morning?
2 When does Sunny Star create problems?
3 What does Sunny Star do when it's angry?
4 What don't you have to do when you use Travel Plus?
5 Why don't you have to get up in the morning?
6 What mustn't you forget when you use Travel Plus?

GRAMMAR

mustn't / don't have to

1 **Complete the sentences from the reviews. Then complete the rule with *mustn't* or *don't have to*.**

1 You _____ do anything. Sunny Star does all the work for you.
2 You _____ forget to switch Travel Plus off at night.

> **RULE:** Use [1]_____ to say 'it's not necessary'.
> Use [2]_____ to say 'don't do it! I'm telling you not to!'

2 **Match sentences 1–2 with a–b.**

1 You don't have to go swimming.
2 You mustn't go swimming.

a There are sharks.
b You can do something else if you prefer.

3 **Complete the sentences with *mustn't* or *don't have to*.**

1 A Dad, I don't want to go to the park with you.
   B No problem, Mike. You _____ be there.
2 A I'm so thirsty.
   B Stop! You _____ drink that!
3 A I'm sorry I can't join you.
   B That's fine. You _____ come.
4 A Sorry, I can't stay. I'm in a hurry.
   B Oh, no problem. You _____ wait for me.
5 A I don't like swimming.
   B We _____ go swimming. We can go to the park.
6 A The neighbour's dog is in the street. You _____ go out.
   B Thanks for telling me. I'm scared of that dog.

Workbook page 65

Pronunciation

Vowel sounds: /ʊ/ and /uː/

Go to page 121.

VOCABULARY
Housework

2.10 Match the words with the photos. Write 1–10 in the boxes. Listen and check. Then listen again and repeat.

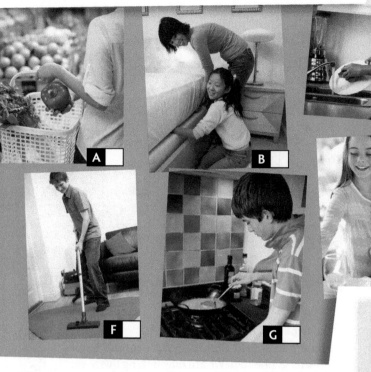

1 vacuum the floor | 2 tidy up | 3 do the ironing
4 do the shopping | 5 set / clear the table
6 do the washing-up (wash up) | 7 make the beds
8 do the cooking | 9 do the washing
10 load / empty the dishwasher

Workbook page 66

SPEAKING

1 **Read the questions. Make notes.**

   1 What do you have to do at home: tidying, shopping, cooking, etc.?
   2 What don't you have to do?
   3 What should parents / children do at home?

2 **Plan what you are going to say. Use these phrases.**

   I have to …   I think / don't think that's fair.

   I don't have to …   I'm quite happy about that.
                       But it would be OK for me to do that.

   I think …   should do the same amount of work.
   It's not fair that …
   Mothers / Fathers should do more work because …

3 **Work in pairs or small groups. Compare your ideas about housework.**

WRITING
A paragraph about housework

Ask your partner these questions and make notes. Then write a paragraph.

1 What do you have to do at home?
2 What don't you have to do at home?
3 When do you have to do housework?
4 What do you feel about this housework?

Kate hates clearing the table, but she has to do it every evening. She also has to vacuum her bedroom floor once a week. She doesn't have to do …

▮ THiNK SELF-ESTEEM ▮
Classroom rules

1 **Write sentences about things students *have to*, *should(n't)* or *mustn't* do.**

   Students have to study for their tests.
   Students should speak English as much as possible.
   Students mustn't leave rubbish on their desks.

2 **SPEAKING Compare your sentences in class. Say what you think.**

   I think it's a good idea / fair / not fair that …

   I think students / teachers / we all should(n't) …

3 **Carry out a vote to agree on the rules for your class. Make a poster, sign it and put it on the wall.**

The treasure hunt

1 🔊 2.11 **Read and listen to the photostory and answer the questions.**

Why can't Ryan come to Luke's house after school?

What's a GPS treasure hunt?

LUKE Come to my house after school.
RYAN Sorry, no chance. I have things to do.
LUKE Oh, yeah? Like what, Ryan?
RYAN Oh, homework and stuff. And I promised to help my dad with the garden. Sorry.
LUKE OK. Never mind.

1

RYAN Hey, come here, Luke. I've found something. It looks like a box. It IS a box!
LUKE What's in it? Gold coins? Diamonds? 'Ladies and gentlemen. We are now talking live to the two lucky boys who found the treasure in the park.'
RYAN You think you're really funny, Luke.
LUKE Absolutely! Come on, open the box!

2

RYAN What do we do now?
LUKE Eat it?
RYAN That sounds like a good idea. But hurry up.
LUKE What do you mean?
RYAN Look. Olivia and Megan are coming. I don't want to share it with them.

3

LUKE Hi, you two.
RYAN So, what are you up to? Using the GPS on your phone to find your way home?
MEGAN No. We're on a treasure hunt.
RYAN Sorry?
MEGAN We're trying to find some treasure. Here in the park. Using the GPS on my phone. It's such good fun!
LUKE Treasure? You mean, like a box with a little surprise in it?
OLIVIA Exactly! Now, can we keep looking?

4

DEVELOPING SPEAKING

2 **Work in pairs. Discuss what happens next in the story. Write down your ideas.**

We think Olivia and Megan find the box. They find ... there.

3 ▶️ **EP4** **Watch to find out how the story continues.**

4 **Answer the questions.**

1 What is Luke worried about?
2 Where does Ryan think Luke is going?
3 What's the problem with the mobile?
4 What does Olivia do to solve the problem?
5 What's the problem for Luke and Ryan?
6 What do the girls find in the box?

PHRASES FOR FLUENCY

1 **Find the expressions 1–5 in the story. Who says them? How do you say them in your language?**

0 no chance   *Ryan*   3 Absolutely. _____

1 ... and stuff. _____   4 So, ... ? _____

2 Never mind. _____   5 ... such good fun _____

2 **Complete the dialogue with the expressions in Exercise 1.**

A Do you want to come round tonight? We can play computer games [1]_____ .

B Sure. I love computer games, they're [2]_____ .

A Of course. And can you bring your new laptop?

B [3]_____ . It's my brother's, too. I can't take it.

A [4]_____ . We can use mine. [5]_____ , is seven o'clock OK?

B [6]_____ ! See you at seven!

WordWise

Expressions with *like*

1 **Complete the sentences from the story with the phrases in the list.**

like | looks like | sounds like | Like what

1 Oh, yeah? _____ , Ryan?
2 It _____ a box. It IS a box.
3 That _____ a good idea.
4 Treasure? You mean, _____ a box with a little surprise in it?

2 **Match the sentences.**

1 This chicken isn't very good.
2 Someone's talking. Who is it?
3 Let's buy her a present.
4 He's a really nice guy.
5 What's that animal?

a Like what? A poster perhaps?
b Yes, he's just like his sister, she's nice too.
c I'm not sure. It looks like a dog, but it isn't.
d That's right. It tastes like fish!
e It sounds like Jim.

3 **Complete the dialogues using a phrase with *like*.**

1 A I really hate tomatoes.
  B I'm _____ you. I hate them, too.

2 A Here's a photo of my sister.
  B Wow. She really _____ you!

3 A We should do some exercise.
  B _____ ? Go for a walk?

4 A Let's go to the cinema.
  B That _____ a great idea.

Workbook page 66

FUNCTIONS
Asking for repetition and clarification

1 **Complete the extracts from the conversations with the words from the list.**

you mean | Sorry? | Like what

LUKE   Come to my house after school.
RYAN   Sorry, no chance. I have things to do.
LUKE   [1]_____ , Ryan?

RYAN   OK, that sounds like a good idea. But hurry up!
LUKE   What do [2]_____ ?

MEGAN   We're on a treasure hunt.
RYAN   [3]_____
MEGAN   A GPS treasure hunt.

2 **Match the expressions in Exercise 1 with their definitions.**

a Say that again.   _____
b What are you trying to say?   _____
c Give me an example.   _____

ROLE PLAY A phone call

Work in pairs. Student A: Go to page 127. Student B: Go to page 128. Take two or three minutes to prepare. Then have a conversation.

8 SPORTING MOMENTS

A

B

C

D

E

F

READING

1 Match the words in the list with the photos. Write 1–6 in the boxes.

1 basketball | 2 horse racing | 3 mountaineering
4 athletics | 5 swimming | 6 tennis

2 Which sport(s) in Exercise 1 has these things?

a ball | a race | a track | water
rope | a net | a match | a rider

3 Name other sports in English.

4 Which sports are popular in your country? Which ones do you like? Write P (popular) and/or L (like) next to each photo.

5 SPEAKING Compare your ideas with a partner.

> *Basketball is popular here but I don't like it very much.*

> *I like tennis and it's very popular here.*

6 Look at the photos on page 75. Answer these questions.

1 Which sports are the stories about?

2 There is something that connects both stories. What is it, do you think?

7 ◀)) 2.12 Read and listen to the article and check your answers.

8 Read the article again. Correct the information in these sentences.

1 The weather in Barcelona was bad.

2 Derek Redmond ran in the 200-metre race.

3 The race organisers tried to help Derek.

4 Derek was running when he crossed the finish line.

5 In 2010, Gerlinde Kaltenbrunner had already tried to climb K2 three times before.

6 Gerlinde was alone on the mountain.

7 The accident happened in the evening.

8 Gerlinde's dream of climbing all of the mountains in the world that are 8,000 metres or higher, is still incomplete.

IF YOU DON'T GIVE UP, YOU CAN'T FAIL ● ● ● ● ●

There are many stories of brave people in sport who didn't give up. Here are two of our favourites.

Derek Redmond

It was the Olympic Games in Barcelona in 1992; the semi-final of the 400 metres. The sun was shining and the crowd were ready for a great race. The British athlete Derek Redmond was a top runner: he had a very good chance of winning a medal.

The race began. At first, Derek was running well. Then, after about 150 metres, he felt a pain in his leg. He fell down on one knee. He had a bad injury and couldn't carry on. The other runners went past him and finished the race.

After about five seconds, Derek got up and started to run again, on one leg only. Some organisers tried to stop him but he kept going. The crowd stood up and started to clap. Then another man came onto the track – Derek's father, Jim. His father put his arm around him and said, 'Derek, you don't have to do this.' Derek replied, 'Yes I do. I have to finish.' And so together they walked the last 50 metres and crossed the line.

When he finally crossed the line, Derek was crying and 60,000 people were cheering him.

Gerlinde Kaltenbrunner

In the summer of 2010, mountaineer Gerlinde Kaltenbrunner was almost at the top of a mountain called K2 in Nepal. She was trying to climb the 8,611-metre mountain for the fifth time, and this time she was climbing with her friend Fredrik Ericsson.

It was about 7 o'clock in the morning and it was snowing a little. The two climbers were getting ready to go up the last 400 metres. Fredrik was trying to tie some rope but he slipped and fell past Gerlinde. He fell 1,000 metres and was killed.

Gerlinde went back to base-camp. K2 was now a very sad place for her, and she thought perhaps she would never climb the mountain.

But there was something very important that she wanted to do: K2 is one of 14 mountains in the world that are 8,000 metres or higher, and her dream was to climb them all.

So in August 2011 she went back to Nepal and K2, and tried again. This time, she got to the top. Her dream was complete.

■ THiNK VALUES ■

Trying, winning and losing

1 **Think about these sentences. Which one do you think is the most important?**

The two stories tell us that …
1 it's important to try to win a race.
2 you shouldn't start a race if you think you can't win.
3 when you start something, you should try to finish.
4 if things go wrong, you should try to keep going.
5 if you try to climb a mountain but don't get to the top, you fail.

2 **SPEAKING** **Work in pairs. Compare your ideas with a partner.**

> *I think number 1 is the most important. What about you?*

GRAMMAR
Past continuous

1 Complete the sentences from the article on page 75 with the words in the list.
Then (circle) the correct words to complete the rule.

run | try | climb | shine

1 The sun _____ in Barcelona.
2 At first, Derek _____ well.
3 Gerlinde _____ with her friend Fredrik Ericsson.
4 Fredrik _____ to tie some rope.

> **RULE:** Use the past continuous to talk about *completed actions / actions in progress* at a certain time in the past.

2 Find more examples of the past continuous in the article on page 75. Then complete the table.

Positive	Negative	Questions	Short answers
I/he/she/it [1] _____ working	I/he/she/it [3] _____ (was not) working	[4] _____ I/he/she/it working?	Yes, I/he/she/ it [6] _____ . No, I/he/she/it [7] _____ (was not).
you/we/they [2] _____ working	you/we/they weren't (were not) working	[5] _____ you/we/ they working?	Yes, you/we/they/ [8] _____ . No, you/we/they [9] _____ (were not).

Pronunciation
Strong and weak forms of *was* and *were*
Go to page 121.

3 Yesterday the sports teacher was late. What were the students doing when he got there? Complete the sentences with the correct form of the verbs in brackets.

0 Lucy <u>_was talking_</u> (talk) on her phone.
1 Daniel and Sophie _____ (play) basketball.
2 Samuel _____ (read) a book.
3 Ken _____ (climb) up a rope.
4 Lisa _____ (dream) about a day on the beach.
5 Andy _____ (look) at his photos on his tablet.

4 Complete the dialogues with the past continuous form of the verbs.

1 A What _____ (you/do) yesterday when we phoned you?
  B I _____ (wait) for my mother in town. And it was horrible because it _____ (rain)!
2 A Why didn't you answer when I phoned you?
  B I _____ (cook) my lunch.
3 A Was it a good game yesterday?
  B Well, the beginning was fine. We _____ (play) well and we _____ (win). But then they scored four goals!
4 A _____ (you/watch) TV when I called last night?
  B No, I wasn't. I _____ (read) a magazine.

> Workbook page 72

VOCABULARY
Sports and sports verbs

1 Match the words in the list with the photos. Write 1–10 in the boxes.

1 sailing | 2 diving | 3 golf | 4 gymnastics
5 rock-climbing | 6 rugby | 7 snowboarding
8 skiing | 9 volleyball | 10 windsurfing

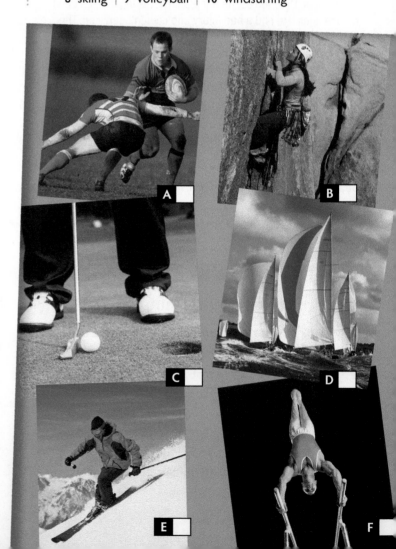

A ___   B ___
C ___   D ___
E ___   F ___

2 Answer the questions.

1 Two of the sports in Exercise 1 have *players* and a *team*. Which ones are they?

2 Seven of the sports in Exercise 1 add *-er* or *-or* for the people who do them. Which ones are they?

3 What do we call someone who does gymnastics?

3 We use different verbs for different kinds of sports. Read the rule and then complete the table with the sports in Exercise 1.

RULE:

play + game (e.g. *football*)
go + *-ing* (e.g. *running*)
do + activity (e.g. *athletics*)

play	*go*	*do*
football	*running*	*athletics*

4 SPEAKING Work in groups. Answer the questions about the sports in Exercise 1.

Which sports …
1 are team sports?
2 are dangerous?
3 are water sports?
4 are in the Winter Olympics?
5 are expensive?
6 are difficult to play or do?

Workbook page 74

LISTENING

1 ◀》2.15 Five teenagers were asked the question: 'How do you feel about sport?' Listen and tick (✓) the sport(s) that each one mentions.

	Gemma	Andy	Tracey	Paul	Ryan
football					
swimming					
running					
skateboarding					
gymnastics					
skiing					
tennis					

2 ◀》2.15 Listen again. Who expresses these ideas? Write the name.

1 I practise a lot. _____
2 I am not competitive. _____
3 I like doing things alone. _____
4 I'm learning another sport. _____
5 I can't do my sport at school. _____

3 SPEAKING Work in pairs. Which of the five teenagers are you like? Tell your partner.

> *I'm like Gemma because I don't really like sport.*

> *I really like running, so I'm like Andy.*

FUNCTIONS
Talking about feelings

1 You are going to answer the question: 'How do you feel about sport?' List some sports you want to talk about.

running, football, swimming, surfing

2 What do you want to say about each sport? Mark them ✓ for positive comments; and ✗ for negative ones.

running ✗   football ✗   swimming ✓   surfing ✓

3 Think about <u>why</u> you put ✓ or ✗. Look at the words and ideas in Vocabulary, Exercise 4. Use these words and / or other words you know.

running ✗ boring   football ✗ team sport
swimming ✓ fun   surfing ✓ difficult and fun

4 Work in pairs. Ask each other: 'How do you feel about sport?'

> *How do you feel about sport?*

> *Well I don't like running because it's boring. But swimming is fun and I love surfing because it's fun and it's difficult to do.*

READING

1 Look at the pictures. What do you think is happening in each one?

A

B

C

D

2 Read the stories and match them with the pictures. Write the numbers 1–4 in the boxes.

3 Read the stories again. Answer the questions.

1 Why does Alan think the story about the bird is funny?

2 Why didn't the girl see the ball coming at her?

3 What happened to the referee?

4 Why did the cyclist lose control of the bike?

4 SPEAKING How funny do you think these stories are? Give each one a number from 0–5 (0 = not funny at all, 5 = very, very funny). Compare your ideas with a partner.

■ TRAIN TO THiNK ■

Sequencing

1 Look at the lists. Put them in a logical order.

1 morning – night – afternoon – evening

2 tomorrow – today – next week – yesterday

3 Saturday – Wednesday – Monday – Friday

4 have lunch – come home – go to school – wake up

5 baby – adult – child – teenager

6 first half – kick-off – half-time – second half

2 SPEAKING Compare your ideas with other students. Are they the same or different?

Your favourite sports FAILS!

1 ALAN Today 4 pm

I saw a really funny thing on YouTube the other day. It was a tennis match. Four people were playing – it was in a big competition. One of the players was hitting the ball when a bird flew in – and the ball hit the bird and it fell to the ground. The players stopped and one of them picked the bird up – they thought it was dead. But suddenly the bird flew away again and they all laughed!

2 JILLY Today 1 pm

I was watching an American football game, a long time ago. There were some girls who were standing at the side of the ground. One player threw the ball really hard – and very badly! One of the girls was looking the other way when the ball hit her. She just didn't see it – and it knocked her over. Everyone was worried; the player went to see if she was OK – then she stood up and laughed and the player gave her a big hug.

3 MARK Today 10 am

I love sumo wrestling – you know, the big Japanese men who wrestle in a small ring. I was watching some on TV, and one wrestler started pushing the other one. He was pushing and pushing and they started to fall over, and the little referee was there behind them – he was trying to get out of the way but then the two men fell on him and he fell out of the ring!

4 PAULA Today 9 am

I went to watch a cycling race the other day. I was standing at the finishing line, and I saw the first cyclist come round the corner to finish the race. At first, he was very happy because he was winning – but he wasn't at the finishing line yet! While he was still cycling, he put his arms up in the air to celebrate. After two seconds, he lost control of the bike. And finally he fell off! He got back on the bike but another cyclist went past him, so in the end he came second. Poor guy – but it was his fault!

GRAMMAR
Past continuous vs. past simple

1 **Look at these sentences from the stories on page 78. Underline the past continuous verb and circle the past simple forms.**

 1 One of the players was hitting the ball when a bird flew in.
 2 One girl was looking the other way when the ball hit her.
 3 He was trying to get out of the way but the two men fell on him.
 4 While he was still cycling, he put his arms up in the air.

2 **Look at the diagram. Which part of the sentence tells us the background action? Which part of the sentence tells us what happened at one moment? Complete the rule.**

*One of the players **was hitting** the ball*

*a bird **flew** in.* ↑

> **RULE:** Use the [1]_____ to talk about background actions in the past, and the [2]_____ for actions which happened at one moment (and sometimes interrupted the background action).

3 **Complete the sentences. Use the past continuous or past simple form of the verbs.**

 0 He _was running_ (run) and he suddenly ___felt___ (feel) a pain in his leg.
 1 The ball _____ (hit) me while I _____ (watch) a bird.
 2 Jenny _____ (sail) with her father when she _____ (see) some dolphins.
 3 He _____ (chase) the ball and he _____ (fall) over.
 4 When I _____ (look) out of the window, it _____ (snow).
 5 The electricity _____ (go) off while we _____ (watch) a match on TV.

4 **Complete the text with the correct form of the verbs.**

A few years ago, in a football match in England between Chelsea and Liverpool, a strange thing happened. Chelsea [1]_____ (win) the match 2–1 and there were about twenty minutes left. Two players – Luis Suárez and Branislav Ivanović – [2]_____ (run) after the ball. While they [3]_____ (try) to get to the ball, Suárez suddenly [4]_____ (take) Ivanović's arm and [5]_____ (bite) it! The referee [6]_____ (not see) it happen so Suárez [7]_____ (continue) playing.

when and while

5 **Look at the sentences in Exercises 3 and 4. Complete the rule.**

> **RULE:** We often use **when** before the past [1]_____ and **while** before the past [2]_____.

6 **Complete the sentences. Use the past continuous for the longer activity and the past simple for the shorter one.**

 0 I _was writing_ (write) an email. My phone _rang_ (ring).
 1 Alex and Sue _____ (watch) a film on DVD. Their friends _____ (arrive).
 2 Marco _____ (have) breakfast. He _____ (have) a great idea.
 3 Cristina _____ (talk) on the phone. Her father _____ (go) out.
 4 They _____ (walk) in the mountains. They _____ (see) strange bird.

7 **Join the sentences in Exercise 6 in two different ways. Use when and while.**
*I was writing an email **when** my phone rang.*
***While** I was writing an email, my phone rang.*

> Workbook page 73

VOCABULARY
Adverbs of sequence

1 **Match the parts of the sentences.**

 1 At first,   a two seconds, he lost control of the bike.
 2 Then   b he was very happy.
 3 After   c he fell off.
 4 Finally,   d he put his arms up to celebrate.

2 **Complete the story with the words in Exercise 1.**

[1]_____ , I was very nervous. [2]_____ the starter fired the gun.

[3]_____ ten seconds, I crossed the finish line and won! I was the Olympic champion!

[4]_____ the photographers took photos of me. [5]_____ an hour, they gave me the gold medal.

[6]_____ , I woke up.

> Workbook page 74

Culture

1 Look at the pictures and answer the questions. Then say what you think the article is about.

Where can you see the following things?
- a marathon race
- an athlete
- spectators
- the finishing line

2 ◀)) 2.16 Read and listen to the article. Match the pictures with the correct Olympic Games.

3 SPEAKING Which Olympic moment do you like most? Which do you not like? Compare your ideas with others in the class.

THE OLYMPIC GAMES – the good and the not-so-good

The Olympic Games takes place every four years and usually there is something special that people never forget. Here are some of those moments from the past – some good, some not so good.

1908 London – the marathon
At the end of the marathon, the man who was winning – Dorando Pietri, from Italy – was very tired and fell down four times. People picked him up and he crossed the line – so of course he didn't win the gold medal because people helped him. But he became very famous.

1960 Rome – a winner with no shoes
The winner of the marathon in Rome was Abebe Bikila from Ethiopia. A lot of other runners (and some of the spectators – the people in the stadium) laughed when they first saw him – he had no shoes. They weren't laughing at the end when Bikila won the gold medal. (He won in 1964 in Tokyo too – but wearing shoes.)

1968 Mexico – a big jump
Mexico City is very high and the air is thin – which was a good thing for some athletes, not so good for others. One special moment was the long jump – Bob Beamon of the USA jumped 8.9 metres. Beamon's jump was the World Record for 23 years.

1996 Atlanta – a bomb
During the 1996 Olympic Games, something very sad happened. A bomb exploded in a park near the Olympic stadium. One person was killed, and 111 people were taken to hospital.

2000 Sydney – the Green Games
The Sydney Olympic Games were called 'The Green Games' because all the buildings (the stadium, the houses for the athletes, etc.) were built to be as friendly as possible to the environment. Many people thought these Olympic Games were the best ever.

2004 Athens – another marathon story
In the men's marathon, after about 35 kilometres, Brazilian Vanderlei de Lima was running very fast. He was first, and the second runner was 40 seconds behind him. But then an Irishman ran out from the crowd and pushed him. Other people in the crowd stopped the Irishman. Then de Lima started to run again. He was smiling when he finished the marathon third – he won the bronze medal.

2012 London – a bottle-thrower
It was the final of the men's 100 metres. All the athletes were ready to start the race. Suddenly a man in the crowd threw a plastic bottle at the athletes. But they were lucky. The bottle didn't hit any of them. The race started. A Dutch woman was sitting next to the man. She grabbed him so he couldn't run away. The woman, Edith Bosch, was a bronze-medal winner in judo at the Games.

A

B

C

4 Read the article again and answer the questions.

Who ...

1 had help to finish the race?
2 raced barefoot?
3 was stopped in the middle of his race?
4 caught a criminal?
5 won gold in two different Olympics?
6 came 3rd in an event at the London Olympics?
7 finished first but didn't get a medal?
8 broke an Olympic record?
9 won a marathon bronze medal?

5 VOCABULARY There are eight highlighted words in the article. Match the words with these meanings. Write the words.

0 took quickly in their hands   _grabbed_
1 the prize given to the athletes that come third in a race at the Olympics _____
2 a 42.2 km race   _____
3 happens   _____
4 the prize given to the winners at the Olympic games _____
5 a competition where athletes run to see who is the fastest _____
6 people who watch a race or game   _____
7 went from one side to the other side _____

WRITING
An article about a sporting event

1 Read Max's article in a school magazine about going to an important tennis match. Answer the questions.

1 Who did Max go with?
2 Who did Max think would win?
3 Who won?
4 What did Max do after the match?

2 Find these words in the article. What does each word describe? Why does Max use them?

0 lucky   _my family_

1 full   _____   4 great   _____
2 excited _____   5 fantastic _____
3 unhappy _____

3 Look at the three paragraphs of Max's article. Match the paragraphs with the contents.

Paragraph 1   a after the event
Paragraph 2   b introduction to the event
Paragraph 3   c details of the event (the match itself)

4 Think of a sports event that you went to or would like to go to. Answer the questions.

1 When is / was the event?
2 Where is / was it?
3 What is / was the atmosphere like (the crowd and the noise, etc.)?
4 What happens / happened at the event? (players / goals / winners, etc.)
5 How did / would you feel after the event? (happy? tired? excited? unhappy?)

5 Write an article for a school magazine (about 120–150 words) about the sports event. Use Max's article and the language above to help you.

SPORTS NEWS

(1) Last Saturday was the final of the women's singles at the Wimbledon Tennis Championships, played (of course) at the Wimbledon Tennis Club. My family were lucky enough to get tickets. When we got there, we went to the court and found our seats. Of course the stadium was full and everyone was very excited. It was brilliant!

(2) At ten to two, the players came out: Marion Bartoli from France and Sabine Lisicki from Germany. At first, I was sure Lisicki was going to win but when the match started, it was clear that I was wrong. Bartoli played really well and after thirty minutes, the first set ended: 6–1 to Bartoli. And twenty-five minutes later, the second set was 5–1 to Bartoli. Lisicki was very unhappy but she started to play better, and soon it was 5–4. Could Lisicki come back? No. Bartoli hit great shots and won the second set 6–4. The crowd stood and clapped and cheered. And then Bartoli got the trophy.

(3) When the match ended, we looked around a bit and then went home. We had a great time. Maybe the match wasn't the most exciting ever, but it was fantastic to see a big sports event 'live'.

THiNK EXAMS

READING AND WRITING
Part 1: Matching
Workbook page 71

1 Which notice (A–H) says this (1–5)? Write the letters A–H.

0 Adults only. ☐ C

1 You don't have to pay if you're eight. ☐

2 You shouldn't leave your car here. ☐

3 The shop closes in the afternoon. ☐

4 You should call for more information. ☐

5 You mustn't swim here. ☐

Please phone for more details. **A**

• Museum •
FREE
to children under nine **B**

You have to be over (18) to watch this film. **C**

Please DON'T park in front of our shop. **D**

OPENING HOURS
9 am – 11.30 am **E**

DANGEROUS DEEP WATER
KEEP OUT **F**

CLOSED on Saturdays **G**

Parking £2 per hour **H**

Part 3: Multiple-choice replies

2 Complete five conversations. Choose the correct answer A, B or C.

0 It's not cold today.
A You mustn't wear shorts.
B You must wear a jacket.
C You don't have to wear a jumper.

1 It's very dark. I can't see anything.
A You need some headphones.
B Here's a torch for you.
C I've got a docking station, if you want.

2 I've got a headache.
A You should go to bed for half an hour.
B You should watch TV.
C You shouldn't get some rest.

3 Let's go sailing tomorrow.
A I can't. I haven't got a bike.
B OK, I've got a ball.
C Sorry, I don't like water.

4 Where were you at 3 pm?
A I am watching TV.
B I walked in the park.
C I was playing basketball.

5 Do you want to go to the cinema?
A No, I have to.
B Sorry. I've got to tidy up.
C Yes, I must.

LISTENING
Part 4: Note taking
Workbook page 79

3 🔊 2.17 You will hear a man asking for information about a football match. Listen and complete each question.

Football match

Day of game: 0 _Sunday_

Game starts: 1 _____

Family ticket: 2 £ _____

Food: 3 Hot drinks and _____

Buy tickets at: 4 Club shop in _____ Street

TEST YOURSELF

VOCABULARY

1 **Complete the sentences with the words in the list. There are two extra words.**

calculator | sailing | remote control | coffee machine | does | headphones
volleyball | up | windsurfing | satnav | make | skiing

1 We're lost. We need a _____ .
2 I have to _____ my bed every morning before I go to school.
3 What a mess. Someone should do the washing- _____ .
4 I love _____ . I've got a small boat and I go every weekend.
5 What is 7% of 270? I need a _____ .
6 I was playing _____ when the ball hit me on the head.
7 Pass me the _____ , please. I want to watch the news.
8 My mum was _____ and she fell over in the snow three times!
9 Dad _____ the cooking in my house.
10 I'm trying to work and your music is too loud. Can you wear _____ ?

/10

GRAMMAR

2 **Complete the sentences with the past simple or past continuous form of the verbs.**

see | walk | stop | eat | find | play

1 She _____ her dog when I saw her.
2 I was tidying my room when I _____ my favourite pen that I lost last week.
3 The docking station _____ working while we were listening to music.
4 We started running when we _____ the bus.
5 I _____ my dinner when the phone rang.
6 We _____ football when Mum called us for dinner.

3 **Find and correct the mistake in each sentence.**

1 My mum and my dad was playing in the sand with my sister.
2 You not have to go if you don't want to.
3 We mustn't run. The train doesn't go for an hour.
4 You must to be careful. It's very dangerous.
5 I played football when I broke my leg.
6 Yesterday the sports shop was sell them for only £15.

/12

FUNCTIONAL LANGUAGE

4 **Write the missing words.**

1 A You _____ have to eat it if you don't want to.
  B Thanks, I don't _____ like it.
2 A I can't come to your house. I've got lots of things to do.
  B Like _____ ?
  A Well, I've got to help my dad _____ the shopping, for a start.
3 A At _____ I was a bit scared but _____ a while I was OK.
4 A What _____ you doing at nine o'clock?
  B I was _____ the washing-up.

/8

MY SCORE /30

22 – 30	
10 – 21	
0 – 9	

THE WONDERS OF THE WORLD

An amazing place

They eat wild animals, plants, berries, nuts and insects. They hunt with bows and arrows. There are lots of dangerous snakes, spiders and scorpions. There are lions, leopards, cheetahs and hyenas. It's one of southern Africa's hottest places, and there is often no water. Then they have to get their water from plants, for example from desert melons. When they are ill, there are no hospitals. The people have to get their medicine from plants too.

They are the San, the last people living in the Kalahari. The San people have another name –'bush people'. Their lifestyle is very simple, but they know more about animals and plants than most people do. The San people live in small groups of 25–50. They live in huts – little 'houses' that they make from wood and grass. There are no schools for the children. Children learn from the older people in the group. There are lots of things they have to learn so that they can live in a dangerous place like the Kalahari. In the evenings, the groups of people often sit around a fire and tell stories. Many of the stories are about animals and how to hunt them.

The Kalahari is a big area of bushland in southern Africa. It has got two parts. There is less rain in the southern part than there is in the northern part, so the south is drier. There are fewer plants and animals there, and it's a lot more difficult for people to live. But when it rains at the end of the summer, the land becomes greener and more beautiful. For a few weeks, there are millions of little flowers and even butterflies! But soon, the grass and the bushes get dry and turn brown. Then life becomes more difficult again for people and animals.

READING

1 Look at the photos. Which of the animals can you name in English?

2 Name other animals in English. Write them down.

3 SPEAKING Work in pairs. Look at the animals on your list. What countries do you think of?

> Pandas come from China.

> You find spiders all over the world.

4 SPEAKING Work in pairs. Look at the photos again and answer the questions.

1 What do the photos show?
2 Where do these people live?
3 What do you think they eat?
4 What dangers are there?
5 What do these people know a lot about?
6 What's interesting for tourists about this place?

5 ◀)) 2.18 Read and listen to the article. Mark the statements **T** (True) or **F** (False). Correct the false information.

1 The bush people get their water from the river.
2 When the San people are ill, they get medicine from a hospital.
3 The bush people teach children important things about living in the Kalahari.
4 The north of the Kalahari is wetter than the south.
5 There are more animals and plants in northern Kalahari.
6 A holiday in the Kalahari is never dangerous.

Every year, thousands of tourists from all over the world visit the Kalahari. They love driving around the bushland in open jeeps. They love watching the wild animals. Their guides are often San bushmen and the tourists love listening to their stories about the wonders of the Kalahari. The tourists stay in small huts called 'lodges'. They have comfortable beds and showers, but there is no electricity in the huts. When they go out of their hut, they have to be very careful. Sometimes there are lions or leopards around!

6 ┃SPEAKING┃ **Work in pairs or small groups. Think about and answer these questions.**

1 Would you like to go to the Kalahari? Why (not)?
2 Are you interested in wildlife? Why (not)?

> I'd love to / I wouldn't like to ... because ...

> I'm (not) interested in ...

> I think it's too dangerous to ... / wonderful to ...

> I love / hate taking photos.
> watching ... / staying in ...

┃THiNK VALUES┃

Valuing our world

1 **Read and tick (✓) the statements that show that the natural world is important.**

1 Why should I want to go on a safari? There's a nice zoo in my city where I can see lots of animals. ☐
2 I want to build a hotel for 800 people in the Kalahari Desert. We can make a lot of money like that. ☐
3 It's great to learn about wild animals. It helps me to understand more about the world. ☐
4 Who needs lions, leopards and hyenas? They're dangerous animals and that's it! ☐
5 I watch a lot of nature programmes on TV. I support a project to save the tiger in India. ☐

2 ┃SPEAKING┃ **Compare your ideas in pairs.**

> Statement 1 shows that the natural world is not important for this person.

> Why do you think that?

> Because the person doesn't want to see wild animals in nature.

> But maybe that's not true. Maybe he or she thinks flying to other places is not good for nature.

GRAMMAR
Comparative adjectives

1 Look at the article on page 84. Find examples of comparisons. Then complete the table on the right.

2 Complete the sentences. Use the comparative form of the adjectives.

1 Africa is _____ (big) than Europe, but _____ (small) than Asia.

2 Be careful with the spiders in the Kalahari. They're _____ (dangerous) than in Europe.

3 Cars these days are _____ (good) quality than they were 30 years ago.

4 Sarah loves wildlife. For her, holidays in the Kalahari are _____ (interesting) than going to the seaside.

5 My sister has got two children. Her son is nine. His sister is two years _____ (young).

6 John is a musician. It's _____ (easy) for him to learn a new instrument than it is for me.

	adjectives	comparative form
short adjectives (one syllable)	small big hot	0 _smaller_ (than) bigger (than) 1 _____
adjectives ending in consonant + -y	happy dry early	happier (than) 2 _____ (than) 3 _____ (than)
longer adjectives (two or more syllables)	attractive beautiful	4 _____ (than) more beautiful (than)
irregular adjectives	bad good far	worse (than) 5 _____ (than) farther / further (than)

Workbook page 82

VOCABULARY
Geographical features

1 🔊 2.19 Label the picture with the words. Write 1–12 in the boxes. Then listen, check and repeat.

1 ocean | 2 hill | 3 mountain | 4 jungle | 5 river | 6 desert | 7 lake | 8 beach | 9 island | 10 forest

2 **SPEAKING** Work in pairs. Ask your partner to close their book and then ask them about the picture.

> What's A?

> I think it's … / I'm not sure if I can remember. Is it … ? / Can you give me the first letter, please?

3 **SPEAKING** Work in pairs. Compare some of the places. Use the adjectives in the list to help you, or use other adjectives.

hot | big | dangerous | high | nice difficult | beautiful | exciting

> A mountain is higher than a hill.

> Yes, and it's more difficult to climb a mountain.

Workbook page 84

LISTENING

1 **Match the things in the list with the photos. Write 1–4 in the boxes.**

1 vultures | 2 a lion and its kill | 3 a spear | 4 an antelope

A

B

C

D

2 🔊2.20 **Listen to an interview with a bushman from the Kalahari. Choose the title that best sums up what he talks about.**

1 Life in the Kalahari
2 Lions, vultures and antelopes
3 A difficult task for a young man
4 Big cats can't run fast when it's hot

3 🔊2.20 **Listen again. For questions 1–5, tick (✓) A, B or C.**

1 Where was PK born?
A in the Kalahari ☐
B in the Sahara ☐
C in Kenya ☐

2 Before a young man can get married, he has to
A do a task. ☐
B find a lion. ☐
C kill an antelope. ☐

3 It's important for the future family that the young man
A kills many lions. ☐
B likes the girl's father. ☐
C has courage. ☐

4 What can show the bushman where the lion is eating?
A antelopes ☐
B vultures ☐
C his future family ☐

5 To take the kill away from the lion you have to
A run faster than the lion can. ☐
B attack the lion with your spear. ☐
C be very quiet and surprise the lion. ☐

GRAMMAR
can / can't for ability

1 **Look at the examples. How do you say these sentences in your language?**

1 A man **can** run even when it's very hot.
2 Lions **can't** do that.

2 **Look at these sentences from the interview. Complete them with can or can't.**

1 How _____ you find a lion and its kill?
2 You _____ get the kill from the lion at night.
3 How _____ you take the meat away from the lion?

3 **Complete the table.**

Positive	I/you/we/they/he/she/it **can** run fast.
Negative	I/you/we/they/he/she/it [1]_____ (**cannot**) run fast.
Questions	[2]_____ I/you/we/they/he/she/it run fast?
Short answers	Yes, I/you/we/they/he/she/it **can**. No, I/you/we/they/he/she/it [3]_____ (**cannot**).

4 **Make sentences with can and can't.**

0 Simon + run fast / – swim fast
   Simon can run fast but he can't swim fast.
1 Matt + drive a car / – fly a plane
   Matt _____
2 Dogs + understand humans / – speak
   Dogs _____
3 I + write emails / – do maths on my laptop
   I _____
4 They + write stories / – spell well
   They _____

▶ Workbook page 82

■ THiNK SELF-ESTEEM ■
Being brave is …

SPEAKING **Think about and answer these questions. Compare your ideas with a partner.**

1 In what situations do people have to show courage?
2 When is it difficult to show courage?
3 Who could be a role model for you in situations where you need to show courage?

People have to show courage when they are in new situations.

It's difficult to show courage when you're scared.

READING

1 Read the article. Where's the world's driest place?

Death Valley, California

Italy

Antarctica

Could you live there?

1 The hottest place on Earth
Death Valley is one of the world's hottest areas, but the place with the record for the highest temperature is El Aziziya in Libya. There, the temperature reached a record of 57.8°C in 1922. Death Valley's highest temperature on record is 56.7°C. That's not a lot cooler!

2 Antarctica – the place with the most weather records
Antarctica is the most fascinating place for extreme weather. It's the world's coldest place. And it's the wettest, but also the driest place. Are you surprised? Well, here are the facts. People cannot live in Antarctica all year round because it's too cold. In 1983 scientists recorded the lowest temperature ever: -89.4°C! It's also the wettest place on earth, but not because it's got the most rain or snow. It's the 'wettest' place because 98% of Antarctica is covered in ice. But it's also the driest place because it never rains there – it only snows! Antarctica holds another record too – there is a place there with the world's thickest ice; it's 2,555 m deep!

3 The world's best and worst weather
So where are the best and worst places in the world for weather? That's the most difficult question. What's good for one person may be bad for another. In 2012 an organisation named 'International Living' tried to answer this – their number 1 for the best weather was Italy, their number 2 was France, and Mexico was number 3! Where do you think your country would come?

2 Read the article again. Answer the questions.

1 Which is hotter, El Aziziya or Death Valley?
2 What place holds the most weather records?
3 Why is it difficult to say where the world's best and worst weather is?

SPEAKING

Work in pairs. Discuss these questions.

1 Which of the facts did you know before?
2 Which of the facts were new to you?
3 Which of the places mentioned would you like to visit most? Why?
4 What's your answer to the question at the end of the article? Give your reasons.

Pronunciation

Vowel sounds: /ɪ/ and /aɪ/
Go to page 121.

WRITING
An email about a place

Imagine you want to tell a friend about the place in the article that you find most interesting. Write an email (100–125 words).

- Choose the place.
- In your email, say:
  – where the place is
  – what's special about the weather there
  – why you think it's interesting

GRAMMAR
Superlative adjectives

1 Put the words in order to make sentences. Check your answers in the article.

1 world's / hottest / is / of / Death Valley / the / places / one
2 for / the / is / most fascinating / Antarctica / extreme / place / weather
3 coldest / the / place / world's / It's
4 the / Where / weather? / are / and / best / for / worst / places

2 Look at the table. Complete the 'adjectives' column with the words in the list. Then complete the comparative and superlative forms.

~~low~~ | fascinating | happy | bad | hot

	adjectives	comparative form	superlative form
short adjectives (one syllable)	0 _low_ high thick	lower 5 _____ 6 _____	the lowest 14 _____ 15 _____
short adjectives ending in one vowel + one consonant	1 _____ wet	hotter 7 _____	16 _____ 17 _____
adjectives ending in consonant + -y	dry 2 _____	8 _____ happier	18 _____ 19 _____
longer adjectives (two or more syllables)	3 _____ difficult extreme	more fascinating 9 _____ 10 _____	the most fascinating 20 _____ 21 _____
irregular adjectives	4 _____ good far	11 _____ 12 _____ 13 _____	the worst 22 _____ 23 _____

3 Complete the sentences. Use the superlative form of the adjectives.

0 It's Cindy's birthday tomorrow. She's _the happiest_ (happy) girl in class.

1 Brazil is _____ (big) country in South America.

2 I had an awful headache this morning. I think I did _____ (bad) test ever.

3 I think email is _____ (good) way of contacting people.

4 We all live a long way from school, but Sam lives the _____ (far).

5 She's great at Maths. She can solve _____ (difficult) puzzles.

Workbook page 83

VOCABULARY
The weather

1 🔊 2.23 **Write the words under the pictures. Listen and check.**

freezing | sunny | rainy | humid | windy | wet | cloudy | dry | warm | foggy | cold | hot

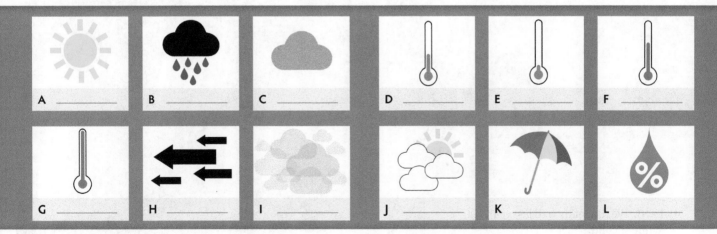

A _____ B _____ C _____ D _____ E _____ F _____

G _____ H _____ I _____ J _____ K _____ L _____

2 Think about the different kinds of weather. Write reasons why you think they can be good.

a sunny day: We can ride our bikes.
a hot day: We can go swimming.
a rainy day: We can play computer games.

3 SPEAKING Work in pairs. Make dialogues with a partner.

What a nice day.

Great idea.

Yes, it's really warm. Let's ride our bikes.

Workbook page 84

The competition

1 🔊 2.24 **Look at the photos and answer the questions. Then read and listen and check your answers.**

What competition is Mr Lane entering?
Why is Megan upset?

1

OLIVIA Hi, guys. Where's Megan?
RYAN She's not with us.
OLIVIA That's strange. I'm sure she said three o'clock.
RYAN Well, it's a nice day. Maybe she went swimming?
LUKE It's only quarter past now. She'll be here in a minute.

2

RYAN Hi, Mr Lane. How are you?
MR LANE I'm OK – a bit busy with this Prettiest Park Competition.
OLIVIA Prettiest Park Competition? What's that?
MR LANE It's a competition to choose the best park in the city.

3

MR LANE We did really well last year. We came second.
RYAN Oh! Well done!
LUKE But this year you want to do better.
MR LANE Of course. I want to show the judges that my park is the most beautiful one in the city.
LUKE Well, good luck. I hope you win.
MR LANE Thanks. It's a lot of work though, and I haven't got much time. And no one to help me, either.

4

MEGAN Sorry I'm late.
OLIVIA No problem. Are you all right?
MEGAN Not really. I was at my granddad's new place. He's pretty upset about having to move. He really misses his garden.
LUKE Does he like gardening, then?
MEGAN Like it?! He loves it!

DEVELOPING SPEAKING

2 Work in pairs. Discuss what happens next in the story. Write down your ideas.

We think the four friends all go to see Megan's granddad's garden.

3 ▶️ **EP5** Watch to find out how the story continues.

4 Put the events in the right order.

a Megan's grandfather meets Mr Lane. ☐

b Megan and Luke go and see her grandfather. **1**

c They admire the garden. ☐

d Megan's grandfather shows the trophy to Megan, Luke, Ryan and Olivia. ☐

e Luke tells Megan's grandfather about the competition. ☐

f Mr Lane and Megan's grandfather work in the park. ☐

PHRASES FOR FLUENCY

1 Find the expressions 1–5 in the story. Who says them? How do you say them in your language?

0 … in a minute. *Luke*   3 No problem. _____

1 Well done! _____   4 Not really. _____

2 … , either. _____   5 … , then? _____

2 Complete the conversations with the expressions in Exercise 1.

1 A I got 87% in the test, Dad.

  B _____ ! Did you study hard for it, _____ ?

2 A Hi, James. I can't talk right now. Sorry. I'll phone you _____ , OK?

  B _____ , Steve. Call me back when you can.

3 A Did you enjoy the film?

  B No, _____ . I didn't like the book very much, _____ .

WordWise
Phrases with *with*

1 Complete the sentences from the story with the phrases in the list.

busy with | to do with me | with us

1 Megan? She's not _____ .

2 I'm a bit _____ the competition.

3 What's this got _____ ?

2 Match the parts of the sentences.

1 You kill the lion ☐

2 It's a paradise ☐

3 We don't offer you a hotel ☐

4 Are you good ☐

a with the biggest rooms.

b with your spear.

c with animals?

d with 200 different kinds of birds.

3 Complete the sentences with the phrases in Exercises 1 and 2.

0 He lives in a house __with__ four bedrooms.

1 Sorry, I can't talk now, I'm _____ my homework.

2 We went to the lake and some friends came _____ .

3 I'm sorry you lost your book, but it hasn't got anything _____ .

4 Have you got a problem with your cat? Talk to John – he's _____ cats.

> Workbook page 84 ▶

1

2

3

FUNCTIONS
Paying compliments

1 Put the words in order to make compliments.

1 a / garden / beautiful / What

2 wonderful / a / garden / It's

3 I / flowers / blue / those / love

2 Work in pairs. Use the photos to make compliments.

> *What a lovely picture!*

10 | AROUND TOWN

OBJECTIVES
....
FUNCTIONS: inviting and making arrangements; talking about plans

GRAMMAR: *be going to* for intentions; present continuous for arrangements; adverbs

VOCABULARY: places in a town; things in town: compound nouns

READING

1 Look at the photos. In which one can you see these things?

1 a **harbour** full of boats

2 a **castle** made of ice

3 a really tall **skyscraper**

2 SPEAKING Work in pairs. Name more places in a town.

station, shop, museum

3 SPEAKING How important are these buildings for a town? Think about who each building is important for and why. Compare your ideas with another pair.

> *A hotel is important for tourists. They need a place to stay.*

4 Work in pairs. Discuss the questions.

1 What is the **population** of your town?

2 Does your town have a **festival** each year?

5 ◀)) 2.25 Read and listen to the blogs. Answer the questions.

1 Where are the writers living now?

2 Where are they going to live?

3 When are they moving?

6 Are the sentences 'Right' (A) or 'Wrong' (B)? If
✳ there is not enough information to answer 'Right' (A) or 'Wrong' (B), choose 'Doesn't say' (C).

1 Alice's mum's job is for a year and a half.

   A Right   B Wrong   C Doesn't say

2 Alice is worried about getting bored in Dubai.

   A Right   B Wrong   C Doesn't say

3 She is excited by the Arab culture.

   A Right   B Wrong   C Doesn't say

4 It gets very cold in Yellowknife.

   A Right   B Wrong   C Doesn't say

5 The Snowking Winter Festival takes place on ice.

   A Right   B Wrong   C Doesn't say

6 Brian really likes sport.

   A Right   B Wrong   C Doesn't say

Alice's World

Today – rain in London. Tomorrow – sun in Dubai! It's time to go. We're going to fly out tomorrow! I am soooo excited! OK, I'm a bit sad to say goodbye to my friends but we aren't going to be in Dubai too long. Mum's contract is only for 18 months. Actually, that's quite a long time but I'm certainly not going to get bored. There are loads of things to do in Dubai. Here's what I'm going to do:

- Go to the top of the Burj al Arab (you know – that building that looks like a ship's sail).
- Visit Port Jebel Ali – the largest man-made harbour in the world.
- Shop – there are zillions of shopping malls there. You can go skiing in one of them.
- Eat Middle Eastern food – I just love it.
- Get into khaliji music – it's amazing.
- Play some golf in the desert (yes, it's possible), and see some tennis at the Dubai tennis stadium.
- And go to school, of course. I'm going to go to the Dubai British School.

I think that's enough to keep me busy!

■ THiNK VALUES ■

Appreciating other cultures

1 **Read and tick (✓) the things you do.**

You are on an exchange trip in a new country for two weeks. Which of these things would you do?

- [ ] Make friends with the local children.
- [ ] Try and find children from your own country who are also on holiday there.
- [ ] Try and learn some of the language.
- [ ] Speak your own language (and hope people understand you).
- [ ] See if the TV shows programmes from your own country.
- [ ] Read the books you brought from home.
- [ ] Visit the museums.
- [ ] Listen to and buy some music by musicians in that country.

The Life of Brian

Big news this week. We're moving! That's right, two months from now it's 'Goodbye Toronto' and 'Hello Yellowknife!'

For those of you who don't know, Yellowknife (population about 19,000) is right at the top of Canada so obviously it's pretty cold – minus 27°C in January! But it gets up to 17°C in the summer.

We're going because Dad's got a new job. He's going to work for a diamond company there.

Anyway the best thing about Yellowknife is every winter there's this really cool festival. It's called the Snowking Winter Festival. Basically, every year they build a really big ice castle on the frozen lake. Then they have loads of concerts and activities for children. They even show films on the walls of the castle. I'm definitely going to that. It's also a really good place to see the Northern Lights. I promise to take loads of photos and put them on my blog.

My sister and I are going to study at the Sir John Franklin High School. It's got a really good theatre so I'm going to do some acting there for sure. There's also a good sports centre too. It's going to be different but I'm sure I'm going to have a good time. And don't worry – I'm not going to stop writing my blog.

2 **SPEAKING** Work in pairs. Decide which of the things in Exercise 1 are good to help you find out more about a different culture. What other things can you think of that are also good to do?

GRAMMAR
be going to for intentions

1 Complete the sentences from the blogs on page 93 with the correct form of the verb *be*.
Use contractions when you can. Then (circle) the correct words to complete the rule.

0   I _'m_____ going to do some acting there for sure.
1   He _____ going to work for a diamond company.
2   We _____ going to be in Dubai too long.
3   My sister and I _____ going to study at the High School.
4   I _____ not going to stop writing my blog.

> **RULE:** Use *be going to* to talk about our intentions for the [1]*future / present*.
> Use the present tense of *be* + *going to* + [2]*base form / -ing form* of the verb.

2 Complete the table.

Positive	Negative	Questions	Short answers
I'm (am) going to play	I'm not (am not) going to play	Am I going to play?	Yes, [5]_____ . No, I'm not.
you/we/they're (are) going to play	you/we/they [1]_____ (are not) going to play	[3]_____ you/we/they going to play?	Yes, you/we/they [6]_____ . No, you/we/they aren't.
he/she/it's (is) going to play	he/she/it [2]_____ (is not) going to play	[4]_____ he/she/it going to play?	Yes, he/she/it is. No, he/she/it [7]_____ .

3 Complete the future intentions with the correct form of the verbs in the list.

~~not watch~~ | take | not fight | not borrow | do | eat

Some family plans – to make us happier!

0   I _'m not going to watch_ so much TV.
1   My parents _____ out more often.
2   We _____ all _____ more exercise.
3   My brother _____ with me anymore.
4   I _____ the dog for a walk every day.
5   My sisters _____ my clothes without asking any more.

4 Look at the table. Tick (✓) the things you are going to do.

tonight	this week	this year
do homework	play sport	write a blog
watch TV	visit relatives	have a holiday
tidy your room	play a computer game	learn something new

5 **SPEAKING** Work in pairs. Ask and answer questions about the activities in Exercise 4.

> *Are you going to watch TV tonight?*   *Yes, I am.*
>
> *What are you going to watch?*   Workbook page 90

VOCABULARY
Places in a town

1 Match the places in the town with the people. Write 1–8 in the boxes.

1 concert hall | 2 car park
3 shopping mall | 4 bus station
5 police station | 6 post office
7 football stadium | 8 sports centre

2 **SPEAKING** Work in pairs. Describe a place from Exercise 1 for your partner to guess.

> *You go here to buy clothes.*

Workbook page 92

LISTENING

1 🔊2.26 **Listen to Tom and Annie. Who is Tom going to the cinema with: Emily or Annie?**

2 🔊2.26 **Listen again and complete the sentences with places in a town.**

1 Tom wants to take Annie to the _____ .
2 There's a new _____ in Bridge Street.
3 The restaurant is next to the _____ .
4 Annie is meeting Emily at the _____ .
5 Annie's relatives want to see the _____ .

3 🔊2.26 **Listen again and complete Annie's diary.**

FRIDAY:	*dinner with Dad*
SATURDAY:	1 _____
	2 _____
SUNDAY:	3 _____

GRAMMAR
Present continuous for arrangements

1 **Look at the examples. Circle the correct options. Then complete the rule with the words in the list.**

1 What *are you doing / do you do* tonight?
2 *I'm having / have* dinner with my dad. *We're going / go* to a restaurant.

present | future | arrangements

> **RULE:** We can use the [1]_____ continuous to talk about [2]_____ for the [3]_____ .

2 **Complete the sentences. Use the present continuous form of the verb.**

0 I *'m going* (go) to Dan's party on Saturday.
1 Oliver _____ (not come) to my house this afternoon.
2 Sara and I _____ (do) our homework together after school.
3 We _____ (not visit) my grandparents on Sunday.
4 _____ your class _____ (go) on a trip next week?
5 My brother _____ (play) in the basketball final on Monday.

3 **Complete the conversation. Use the present continuous form of the verbs in the list.**

not do (x2) | go | buy | meet | do (x2) | play

KENNY What [1]_____ you _____ this afternoon?
OLIVIA Nothing. I [2]_____ anything.
KENNY Paul and I [3]_____ football. Do you want to come?
OLIVIA OK. Can I invite Tim? He [4]_____ anything either.
KENNY Sure. And what about your brother? [5]_____ he _____ anything?
OLIVIA Yes, he [6]_____ shopping with my mum. They [7]_____ his birthday present.
KENNY OK. Well, we [8]_____ Jack, Adam, Lucy and Julia at the park at two.
OLIVIA OK. See you at two, then. `Workbook page 90` ➤

FUNCTIONS
Inviting and making arrangements

1 **Complete the sentences.**

Inviting	[1]_____ _____ like to go the cinema with me? [2]_____ _____ want to go to the cinema with me?
Accepting	I'd [3]_____ to. That would be great.
Refusing	I'm sorry. I [4]_____ . I'm busy.

2 **Work in pairs. Take turns to invite your partner to do these things.**

watch DVD | go theatre | play tennis
go burger bar | come your house

3 **Think of three arrangements and write them in your diary.**

Saturday	Sunday
morning:	morning:
afternoon:	afternoon:

4 **Can you complete your diary? Walk around the classroom and:**

1 invite people to do things with you.
2 find things to do when you're free.

> *Would you like to go to a football match with me on Saturday afternoon?*

> *I'd love to.*

READING

1 Look at the photos. What problem does each one show?

2 Read the letters page and match the problems with the photos. Write 1–4 in the boxes.

A

B

C

D

Our Town:

What's wrong and what can we do about it?

1 Our town looks a mess and that's not good for tourism. I hate the litter in our streets. Why can't people put it in the bins? It's not difficult. We need to educate people quickly. We need more litter bins and billboards saying 'Don't drop it – Bin it!' and things like that.

We also need to punish people who drop litter. I think they should spend a day picking it up.

Charlie, 14

2 People always complain about the kids in our town. They don't like us hanging out in the shopping centre. They say they don't feel safe. But they're wrong. We never cause trouble. We only meet up there because there's nowhere for us to go. It's not easy being a kid. We need more things for young people to do and more places for us to go. A youth club would be great. There are lots of empty buildings in our town centre. They could use one of them.

Mack, 15

3 The biggest problem in our town is the cars. There are too many cars on our roads and the drivers don't care about the pedestrians. They drive really fast. Some of them don't even stop at zebra crossings! I ride my bike everywhere and I just don't feel very safe, even when I'm in a cycle lane. We can stop this problem easily. Let's get more speed cameras to catch these fast drivers and then stop them from driving in our town.

Pauline, 15

4 People like to complain about the graffiti on the shops in the high street. They think it's ugly. I agree that a lot of it is. But if you look closely some of this art is really good. Some of these people paint really well. Why don't we use them to make the town more attractive? I think we should create graffiti walls where these artists can show off their art. Maybe this will stop the problem of them doing it illegally.

Paris, 13

3 Read the letters page again. Answer the questions.

1 What does Charlie think people who drop litter should do?

2 What does Mack think young people need in the town?

3 What does Pauline want to stop?

4 What does Paris think will help stop the graffiti problem?

■ TRAIN TO THiNK ■
Problem solving

1 **SPEAKING** Work in pairs. Read and discuss the problem.

The young people in your town aren't happy. They say there is nothing to do.

Make a list of suggestions to help solve this problem.

have a music festival
build a skateboard park

2 Think about your suggestions. What are the advantages and disadvantages of each one?

Suggestions	😊	😞
music festival	*young people love music / fun*	*noisy / make a mess / expensive*

3 **SPEAKING** Decide which suggestion you think is the best. Compare your ideas with the rest of the class.

> *We think a musical festival is the best idea because all young people love music. It's also a lot of fun.*

GRAMMAR
Adverbs

1 **Look at the sentences from the letters page on page 96. Underline the adjectives and circle the adverbs.**

0 They drive really fast.
1 We can stop this problem easily.
2 It's not easy being young.
3 Let's get more speed cameras to catch these fast drivers.
4 We need to educate people quickly.
5 Some of this art is really good.
6 Some of these people paint really well.

2 **Complete the rule.**

> **RULE:** To form adverbs:
> ● add ¹_____ to regular adjectives (e.g. *quick → quickly*).
> ● delete the 'y' and add ²_____ to adjectives ending in -y.
> Some adjectives have irregular adverb forms.
> e.g. *fast → fast   good → ³_____*
> Adverbs usually come immediately after the object of the verb or the verb (if there is no object). *He plays tennis well.* NOT *He plays well tennis.*

3 **Complete the sentences. Choose the correct words and write them in the correct form.**

0 His car was really _*fast*_ . He won the race _*easily*_ . (easy / fast)
1 Her French is very _____ . She speaks really _____ . (good / fluent)
2 It's not _____ . You need to do it very _____ . (careful / easy)
3 We need to walk _____ . I don't want to be _____ . (late / quick)
4 I did my homework _____ . I was really _____ . (tired / bad)
5 He drives really _____ . I get quite _____ in the car with him. (scared / dangerous)

Workbook page 91

VOCABULARY
Things in town: compound nouns

1 **Choose a word from A and a word from B to make things you can find in a town. Look at the letters on page 96 to help you.**

A zebra | youth | speed | graffiti cycle | litter | bill | high

B wall | street | camera | bin | lane | crossing | board | club

2 **Complete the sentences with the words in Exercise 1.**

0 Slow down. There's a _*speed camera*_ just ahead.
1 I really like that _____ advertising the new Italian restaurant in town.
2 Don't drop your paper on the floor. There's a _____ behind you.
3 Don't try and cross the road here – there's a _____ just down there.
4 We live in a flat above one of the shops in the _____ .
5 The new _____ is really popular. Loads of people are painting on it.
6 I ride my bike to school. There's a _____ from outside my house all the way there.
7 We go to the _____ every Friday night. I usually play table tennis and chat with my friends there.

Workbook page 92

Pronunciation

Voiced /ð/ and unvoiced /θ/ consonants

Go to page 121.

Culture

1 Look at the photos. What do you think a ghost town is?

2 Read the article quickly. Where are these towns?

3 🔊 2.29 Read the article again and listen. Mark the sentences T (true) or F (false).

1 Kolmanskop was once a very rich town.
2 The UFO buildings are a popular tourist attraction in Taipei.
3 Fordlândia became a problem because there was nowhere for the factory workers to live.
4 The Ford family sold Fordlândia for $20 million.
5 They closed Centralia because of an accident.
6 It still isn't safe to visit Centralia today.

Ghost Towns around the World

We build towns for people to live in. But what happens when they don't want to live in them any longer? All over the world there are ghost towns, towns where people don't live any more. Here are a few.

In 1908, many Germans arrived in Luderitz in the southern African country of Namibia. They wanted to look for diamonds and they found a lot. With the money from the **diamonds** they built the town of Kolmanskop. It had lots of beautiful buildings, a hospital, a school, and even a theatre. But when there weren't any more diamonds, they left the town. These days the only things that visitors to Kolmanskop see are empty buildings and a lot of **sand**.

In 1978, a **building company** started building a holiday **resort** in the Sanzhi District of New Taipei City. For the next two years they built a lot of round buildings. They didn't look like normal houses, but more like spaceships. People called them the 'UFO houses'. In 1980, they stopped building the houses because there wasn't enough money and for 28 years the resort was a ghost town. However, no one can visit this city today because in 2008 they **demolished** all the buildings. All we can see now are photos of these strange looking houses.

In Northern Brazil, there is the ghost town of Fordlândia. In 1928, Henry Ford – famous for his cars – decided to build a big factory there to make car tyres. He also built houses for the workers and their families. Unfortunately, the weather in the area wasn't good for growing the trees they needed to

make tyres. Ford tried to make the city a success but it was difficult. In 1945, his grandson Henry Ford II sold Fordlândia. The company lost $20 million. The empty buildings of the town are still there today.

About 70 years ago, Centralia was a busy town in Pennsylvania, USA. It had five hotels, seven churches and 19 big stores. In 1962, a fire started under the town at an old **mine**. They spent millions of dollars trying to stop it but that didn't work. It became too dangerous to live there and everyone had to leave the town. These days a sign across the road to the town tells people to 'stay out'. The fire is still burning today.

4 VOCABULARY **There are six highlighted words in the article. Match the words with these meanings. Write the words.**

0	very expensive stones	*diamonds*
1	destroyed	_____
2	a company that makes houses	_____
3	a small holiday village or town	_____
4	you find a lot of it on beaches and in the desert	_____
5	holes in the ground from where substances such as coal, metal and salt are removed	_____

5 SPEAKING **Work in pairs. Discuss.**

1 Imagine you are going to make a film set in one of these towns. Think about:
- What kind of film is it? (horror, love, science fiction?)
- What's the story about briefly? (It's about a ...)
- Who is going to star in your film? (It's going to star my favourite actors ...)

2 Present your ideas to the group and vote on the best idea.

WRITING
An informal email

1 **Read the email. Answer the questions.**

1 Where is Emily going to spend her summer holidays?
2 What is she going to do there?

2 **Find these expressions in the email. Use them to answer the questions below.**

Guess what? | You won't believe it. | I can't wait. By the way, ... | Anyway, ...

1 Which two expressions do we use to change topic?
2 Which two expressions do we use to introduce some surprising news?
3 Which expression means 'I'm really excited'?

3 **Look at paragraphs 1 and 2 of Emily's email. Match the functions with the paragraphs. Write a–d.**

Paragraph 1: _____ and _____
Paragraph 2: _____ and _____

a Describe the city   b Give news
c Ask how your friend is   d Talk about your plans

4 **What is the function of paragraph 3?**

5 **Which paragraph answers these questions?**

a What famous buildings are there in Sydney?
b What's your news?
c How long are you going to stay in Sydney?
d What's the weather like in Sydney?
e What are you going to do in Sydney?
f Where are you going?

6 **Imagine you are going to spend your next holiday in a famous city. Write an email (about 100–120 words) to your friend telling her the news.**

- Use the questions in Exercise 5 to help you.
- Use some of the language in Exercise 2.

To: luckyluke@writeme.co.uk
Subject: Exciting news!

Hi Luke,

[1] How are you? I hope you're not studying too hard. Don't worry, there are only two more weeks of school. Anyway, I'm writing because I've got some really cool news. You won't believe it. Mum and Dad are taking me to Sydney for the summer. Sydney, Australia! I can't wait.

[2] So I did some research on the Internet. It looks like a really amazing place. Of course, there's the famous harbour with the bridge and the Opera House but there are so many other great things to do there. I'm definitely going to hang out on Bondi Beach. And guess what? Mum's going to buy me some surfing lessons. I'm going to be a surfer! We're going to be there for the whole of August. It's winter there but I think the Australian winter is hotter than our summer. So that's it – my big news. What do you think?

[3] By the way, Dad says we're going to be in Bangor next weekend. Is there any chance we can meet up? Let me know.

Love

Emily

▌THiNK EXAMS ▌

READING AND WRITING

Part 2: Multiple-choice sentence completion

1 **Read the sentences about holiday plans. Choose the best word (A, B or C) for each space.**

0 On Monday we're _____ to Rio de Janeiro.
  A to fly   Ⓑ flying   C fly

1 It's one of the _____ beautiful cities in the world.
  A most   B more   C less

2 The weather there is lovely. It's usually hot and very _____ .
  A freezing   B foggy   C sunny

3 We're _____ to visit my uncle and his family in Brazil.
  A going   B go   C to go

4 I'm also a bit scared because I _____ speak Portuguese.
  A can   B not   C can't

5 Mum says I shouldn't worry, because my cousins all speak English very _____ .
  A well   B good   C badly

Part 7: Open cloze   Workbook page 89 ▶

2 **Complete the text about Llandudno. Write ONE word for each space.**

LISTENING

Part 5: Note completion   Workbook page 79 ▶

3 🔊 **2.30** **You will hear some information about a shopping centre. Listen and complete each question.**

White River SHOPPING CENTRE

● There are over (0) __300__ shops.

● There are restaurants and a (1) _____ on the fifth floor.

● Parking costs (2) £_____ every hour.

● Buses leave for the city centre every (3) _____ .

● Shops close at 5.30 pm every day except (4) _____ .

My name **(0)** __is__ Hugo and I would like to tell you about the town where I live. It's **(1)** _____ the north of Wales and it's called Llandudno. That's probably **(2)** _____ unusual name for you, because it's a Welsh name. Here in Wales, we have our own language. I **(3)** _____ born here and so I speak Welsh really **(4)** _____ .

Llandudno is **(5)** _____ most beautiful town in Wales. Well, that's what I think. It's by the sea and we have lots of beaches. They're **(6)** _____ sandy but have lots **(7)** _____ small stones on them. You **(8)** _____ swim in the sea if you want to, but it's quite cold most of the year.

There are lots of things to do in Llandudno. There **(9)** _____ parks and there's a small mountain where you can take a chair lift to a café at the top. There's a really good concert hall and lots of great bands play here. There's **(10)** _____ a youth club that I go to every Friday night with my friends.

VOCABULARY

1 **Complete the sentences with the words in the list. There are two extra words.**

windy | zebra | lake | hall | mountains | bin | island | lanes | cloudy | sunny | station | house

1 It's very _____ today. You can't see the sun at all.
2 We live on a small _____ . There is sea all around us.
3 Mum and Dad are going to the concert _____ tonight. They're very excited.
4 It's one of the highest _____ in the world and it took the climbers three days to get to the top.
5 It's so _____ that my hat just blew off my head.
6 Don't try and cross the road here. There's a _____ crossing just up there.
7 It's easy to get about town on a bike because there are cycle _____ everywhere.
8 I lost my wallet in the city centre. I went to the police _____ but they didn't have it.
9 Put your rubbish in the litter _____ over there.
10 We went fishing on the _____ but we didn't catch anything.

/10

GRAMMAR

2 **Put the words in order to make sentences.**

1 going / She's / nine / to / me / at / phone
2 Monday / We're / morning / on / leaving
3 homework / carefully / her / did / very / She
4 keys / I / I / remember / my / where / can't / left
5 the / It's / day / hottest / of / year / the
6 than / It's / mine / car / expensive / a / more

3 **Find and correct the mistake in each sentence.**

1 I speak badly French.
2 This is the more popular sport in the world; everybody likes it.
3 I had a lot of presents. But the one most I liked was a blue watch from my mother.
4 She plays tennis very good.
5 He's ten and he still can't to ride a bike.
6 We are to meeting him at nine o'clock.

/12

FUNCTIONAL LANGUAGE

4 **Write the missing words.**

1 A _____ a horrible day!
  B Yes, _____ stay inside and watch TV.
2 A What are you _____ later?
  B Nothing. Why?
  A _____ you want to go skateboarding with me?
3 A _____ you like to come to my house for dinner on Friday?
  B I'd _____ to. Thanks.
4 A _____ what?
  B What?
  A Mum's taking me to Disneyland Paris this summer. I _____ wait!

/8

MY SCORE **/30**

| 22 – 30 |
| 10 – 21 |
| 0 – 9 |

11 | FUTURE BODIES

READING

1 Label the picture with the words in the list. Write 1–12 in the boxes.

1 arm | 2 leg | 3 mouth | 4 muscle | 5 finger | 6 foot
7 ear | 8 eye | 9 toe | 10 hair | 11 bone | 12 thumb

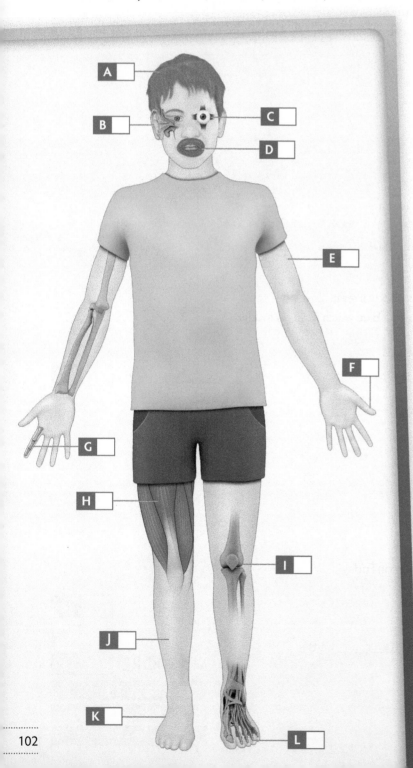

2 Write the words from Exercise 1 in the correct column.

Body	Face
arm	mouth

3 SPEAKING Work in pairs. Discuss the questions.

Which parts of the body do you use when you:
- read a book?
- play football?
- watch television?
- make a phone call?
- eat a meal?
- walk to school?

> When you read a book you use your hands and your eyes.

4 Look at the picture on page 103 and the title. What do you think the article will be about? Choose one of the following.

1 What we want to look like in the future.
2 What the human body will be like in the future.
3 How we can change our bodies if we want.

5 ◀)) 2.31 Read and listen to the article and check your ideas.

6 Read the article again and answer the questions.

1 What is the most important reason why our bodies will change in the future?
2 Why will people be taller?
3 Why will people get weaker?
4 What will happen to eyes and fingers?
5 Why will we have one less toe?
6 Why won't people have so much hair on their bodies?

Changing bodies

A long time ago, people were very different from the way we are now. For example, if you find a really old house somewhere, you'll see that the doors are usually much lower than they are today. Why? Because hundreds of years ago, people were shorter. Over time, the human body changes to adapt to a new way of life.

Can we expect the human body to change in the future? For sure. And the main reason is that we have more and more technology, and it is changing how we live.

What kind of changes can we expect? Well, no one can be 100 per cent sure, but here are some possibilities.

1 Let's start with the example above. Humans are now ten centimetres taller than 150 years ago. So, in the future, people will probably be even taller. Most of us now have much better food than people in the past – and so we grow more.

2 We'll get weaker in more than one way. The most important way is that our muscles will not be as strong as now because we won't do a lot of physical work.

3 We are already using our feet less, and our hands more (think about computers and tablets and so on.) So we can expect that our legs will get shorter and our feet smaller, and at the same time, our fingers will get longer. And our fingers and our eyes will both get better, because they'll have to do more work together.

4 Now, what about the mouth? It'll get smaller, perhaps, because technological improvements will mean that we don't need to talk so much – and also because our teeth will get smaller (so mouths don't need to be so big to keep them in).

5 Here's a good one – it's very possible that people will have four toes, not five. The little toe really isn't needed any more (people who lose them don't miss them) so it will probably disappear some time in the future.

6 And last but not least – people won't have as much hair on their bodies as now, as we don't need it to keep ourselves warm any more.

Will all these things happen? And if so, when? These are questions that no one can answer for sure.

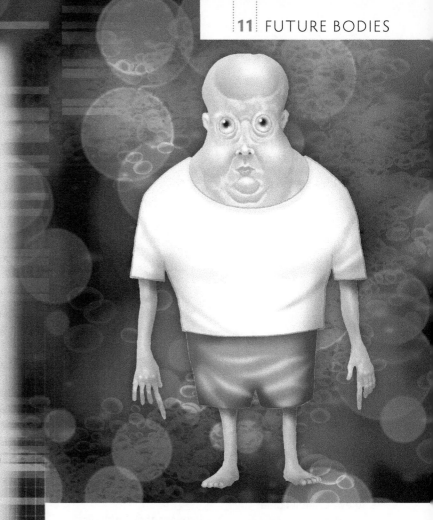

■ THiNK VALUES ■

Exercise and health

1 **Read the sentences. Give each one a number from 1 to 5 (1 = doesn't give a lot of importance to health and 5 = gives a lot of importance to health).**

1 ☐ You should do regular exercise to make sure your muscles are strong.

2 ☐ It's OK to spend a lot of time sitting in front of the television.

3 ☐ A wonderful thing to do is go for long walks in the fresh air.

4 ☐ Using a computer and writing text messages gives your hands and arms exercise.

5 ☐ You don't have to do sport to be healthy and keep fit.

6 ☐ It's a good idea to do a lot of simple exercise (for example, use the stairs and don't take the lift).

2 **SPEAKING Work in small groups. Talk about health and exercise.**

1 Together, decide the number that the group is going to give to each of the sentences in Exercise 1.

2 Together, decide on and write another sentence that shows how the group feels about health and exercise.

3 Compare your ideas with other groups.

GRAMMAR
will / won't for future predictions

1 Look at the sentences from the article on page 103. Complete with *will* / *'ll* / *won't*. Then complete the rule.

1 Our fingers _____ get longer.
2 They _____ have to do more work together.
3 Our muscles _____ be as strong as now, because we _____ do a lot of physical work.

> **RULE:** Use ¹_____ (*will*) or ²_____ (*will not*) + base form of the verb to make predictions about the future.

2 Complete the table.

Positive	Negative
I/you/we/they/he/she/it ¹_____ (will) come	I/you/we/they/he/she/it ²_____ (will not) come

Questions	Short answers
³_____ I/you/we/they/he/she/it come?	Yes, I/you/we/they/he/she/it ⁴_____. No, I/you/we/they/he/she/it ⁵_____ (will not).

3 Complete the conversation. Use *'ll*, *will* or *won't* and a verb from the list.

~~get~~ | stay | go | see | give | be | help

ALICE   Oh, Mark, it's the French test tomorrow! I hate French. I'm sure I ⁰ *won't get* the answers right!

MARK   Don't worry, you ¹_____ fine! You got a good result in your last test.

ALICE   Yes, but this is more difficult. I really don't feel well. Maybe I ²_____ to school tomorrow. I ³_____ in bed all day.

MARK   That ⁴_____ you. The teacher ⁵_____ you the test on Wednesday.

ALICE   You're right. But what can I do?

MARK   Look, why don't I come round to your place this afternoon after school? We can do some French together. You ⁶_____ that it's not so difficult.

ALICE   Oh, thanks, Mark.

4 SPEAKING Work in pairs. Act out the conversation in Exercise 3.

Workbook page 100

> ## Pronunciation
> The /h/ consonant sound
> Go to page 121.

VOCABULARY
Parts of the body

1 Match the words with the photos. Write numbers 1–10 in the boxes.

1 ankle | 2 back | 3 elbow | 4 knees | 5 lips | 6 neck | 7 shoulder | 8 stomach | 9 throat | 10 tongue

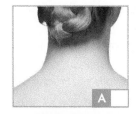
A

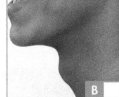
B

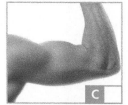
C

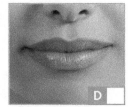
D

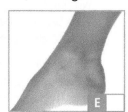
E

F

G

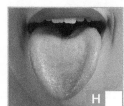
H

I

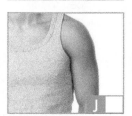
J

2 ◀))2.34 Listen and match the speakers (1, 2 and 3) with the pictures. Write numbers 1–3 in the boxes.

A

B

C

Workbook page 102

LISTENING

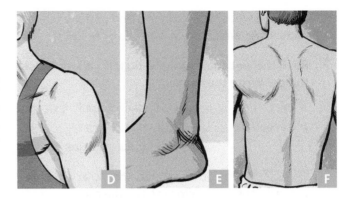

1 Look at the pictures A–C. Answer these questions for each one.

1 Who are the two people?
2 Where are the two people?

2 🔊2.35 Listen to three conversations. Match the pictures with the conversations. Complete the table. Write A, B or C in the 'Speakers' column and D, E or F in the 'Problem' column.

	Speakers (A, B, or C)	Problem (D, E, or F)
Conversation 1		
Conversation 2		
Conversation 3		

3 🔊2.35 Listen again. Mark the statements T (true) or F (false).

1 Katie hurt her shoulder while she was watching skateboarding.
2 When Katie fell, it wasn't a bad fall.
3 David's ankle hurts all the time.
4 David's mother wants to take him to the doctor.
5 Sam didn't tell his parents about his back.
6 Molly wants to take Sam to see the doctor at school.

4 Who said these things? Match the sentences with the speakers.

1 Are you all right?   a the doctor
2 Does it hurt?   b David's mother
3 What's the matter?   c Sam
4 It hurts a bit.   d Molly
5 My shoulder hurts.   e David
6 I've got backache.   f Katie

SPEAKING

Work in pairs. Choose one of the pictures above (A, B or C) in Exercise 2. Role play the conversation.

1 Decide who will be each person in the picture.
2 Choose a different part of the body from the conversation you heard for your picture (example: for Picture A, choose 'head' not 'back').
3 Have a conversation.
4 Now choose another picture. Change roles.

◼ THiNK SELF-ESTEEM ◼

Getting help

1 Read and tick (✓) the sentences that are true for you.

1 ☐ I don't like going to the doctor and so I don't go.
2 ☐ If I have a problem, I don't like telling other people about it.
3 ☐ If I don't feel well, I tell someone.
4 ☐ I don't want other people to worry about me.
5 ☐ It's OK to get help from people around you.
6 ☐ It's important to go to the doctor if you often have the same health problem.

2 SPEAKING Compare your ideas in class.

3 Who can you talk to about these problems?

1 a headache   3 difficult homework
2 a problem at school   4 a problem with a friend

LOOK!

stomach ache   ear ache   headache   toothache

READING

1 Read the webchats. Write a name under each picture: Arlene, Pete, Susie, Julia or Mike.

2 Read the webchats again. Who talks about these things? Write the names.

1 eyes   _____   3 dangerous things _____

2 a vegetable _____   4 making faces _____

                    5 making a noise _____

3 **SPEAKING** Do you know any more 'crazy' things that adults say to children? Tell the class.

A _____

B _____

C _____

D _____

Crazy things that parents say to their kids ✕

 Arlene
Now I'm eighteen, I can look back at all those happy days when I was a kid at home! And I remember the things that my mum and dad said to me again and again. For example: when my sister and I were making a noise, my father always said, 'If I have to come over there, you won't be happy to see me!' lol. Did your parents ever say things like that to you?

👍 LIKE · COMMENT · SHARE

Pete
Oh of course! My little brother and me, we loved TV and we sat and watched it for hours every day. And my mum always looked at us and said, 'If you watch TV all the time, you'll get square eyes.' Well, we watched a lot of TV and our eyes are still normal. haha!

Susie
You reminded me, Pete. My dad always said, 'If you sit too close to the TV, you'll go blind.' But he had another favourite too (I think he was always worried about our eyes, for some reason) – he said, 'If you eat all your carrots, you'll see in the dark.' I really like carrots – I ate them when I was a kid and I eat them now – but I still can't see in the dark!

E _____

Julia
I always liked doing dangerous things – you know, climbing trees and things. And my dad said, 'If you fall you'll break your leg.' And he always added, 'And when you break your leg, don't come running to me for help!' I didn't understand the joke for years!

Mike
Nice one, Julia! OK here's another one, and I think every child in the world hears this. If I was angry or upset, I always made a face, and my mum said, 'If you go on making that face, the wind will change and your face will stay like that forever!' That's the only one I remember – but as soon as I think of others, I'll send them to you!

GRAMMAR
First conditional

1 Match the parts of the sentences. Check your answers in the webchats. Then complete the rule and the table. Choose the correct words.

1 ☐ If you eat all your carrots,

2 ☐ If I have to come over there,

3 ☐ If you fall,

a you won't be happy to see me.

b you'll break your leg.

c you'll see in the dark.

RULE: Use the first conditional to talk about ¹possible / certain events and their ²present / future results.

If clause	Result clause	
If + present simple,	³_____ (*'ll*) ⁴_____ (*won't*)	+ base form

It is possible to put the result clause first:
If you fall, you'll hurt yourself. OR
You'll hurt yourself if you fall.

2 Put the words in order to make sentences.

0 see Jane, / If / tell / I / I'll / her

If I see Jane, I'll tell her.

1 my parents / I'm / will / If / late, / be angry

2 I / bring it / I'll / to school tomorrow / If / remember,

3 you'll / Jake / come / If / you / meet / to the party,

4 rain tomorrow / if / the / it / doesn't / We'll / to / beach / go

5 the concert / if / tonight / I / don't / I / won't / feel better / go / to

3 Complete the first conditional sentences with the correct form of the verbs.

0 If Kate ___*gives*___ (give) me some help, I ___*'ll finish*___ (finish) my homework in an hour.

1 You _____ (not meet) anyone if you _____ (not go out).

2 I _____ (come) to your party if my mum _____ (say) I can.

3 If Ken _____ (not want) his ice cream, I _____ (eat) it.

4 Susan _____ (be) angry if she _____ (hear) about this.

5 If we _____ (buy) hamburgers, we _____ (not have) enough money for the film.

ROLE PLAY

Work in pairs. Student A: Go to page 127. Student B: Go to page 128. Ask and answer the questions.

Workbook page 101

Time clauses with *when* / *as soon as*

4 Read the two sentences and answer the questions. Then complete the rule with *will* and *present simple*.

When we get to school, I'll take you to see the nurse.

As soon as I think of other examples, I'll tell you.

1 What is the difference between *when* and *as soon as*?

2 Do *get* and *think* refer to the present or future?

RULE: In sentences about the future, we use the
1_____ form after *if* or *when* or *as soon as*, and
2_____ + base form of the verb in the main clause.

5 Complete the sentences. Use the verbs in the list.

finish (x2) | get (x2) | arrive

1 As soon as I _____ my exam results, I'll phone you.

2 When I _____ home, I'll check my messages.

3 The party will start as soon as my friend _____ with the music!

4 When the game _____ we'll go and have a pizza.

5 I'll lend you the book as soon as I _____ reading it.

Workbook page 101

VOCABULARY
when and *if*

1 Match sentences 1 and 2 with the explanations.

1 **When I see Martin,** I'll give him your message.

2 **If I see Martin,** I'll give him your message.

a It is possible that I will meet Martin.

b I know that I will meet Martin.

2 Complete the sentences with *if* or *when*.

0 I can't talk to you now. I'll phone you ___*when*___ I get home.

1 A What are you doing tomorrow?

 B _____ there's a good film on, I'll probably go to the cinema.

2 I'm not sure if I want to go to the party tonight. But _____ I decide to go, I'll phone you.

3 It's too hot to go for a walk now. Let's go out in the evening, _____ it's cooler.

4 You can watch some TV _____ you finish your homework, and not before!

5 It's the football final tonight. I'll be very happy _____ my team wins.

Workbook page 102

LISTENING AND WRITING
A phone message

1 Which of these things do you NOT need to write down if you take a phone message? Mark the things with a cross (✗).

1 the name of the caller ☐

2 the telephone number of the person who takes the message ☐

3 the name of the person who the message is for ☐

4 the telephone number of the caller ☐

5 what the caller wants ☐

2 ◀))2.36 Listen to a telephone conversation. Complete the message.

Message from: 1_____

For: 2_____

Message: *she needs* 3_____ .

Please 4_____

Number to call: 5_____

The phone call

1 🔊2.37 **Read and listen to the photostory and answer the questions.**

Why is Megan's father stressed?

Who phones Megan while she's in the park?

OLIVIA Aw, look!

LUKE Looks like they're having a good time.

WOMAN Jason?! You stop that. Do you hear me? Stop it!

RYAN What did you say, Luke?

OLIVIA Well, we all know what that's like – your parents, shouting at you.

1

MEGAN Oh, don't, please! The last couple of days …

RYAN What?

MEGAN Oh, my dad. He's really stressed. He's got a big business meeting he has to attend, out of town tomorrow and Friday.

LUKE Something important?

2

MEGAN I suppose so. I don't know.

RYAN Well, I think you *should* know. I mean, he's your father, right? Family and stuff.

MEGAN Yeah, yeah. Whatever. But I know one thing: he shouts at me all the time. Everything I do is wrong.

OLIVIA Poor you.

WOMAN Jason! I told you – don't do that! If I have to go over there …

MEGAN Just like that. Another few years and I can leave home! I can't wait!

3

OLIVIA Just think, Megan. You'll be a mother too one day. Then you'll remember this.

RYAN That's right. And when we're parents, we'll be just the same as our parents. Wait and see.

MEGAN Hello? Oh, hello, Dad. What is it? I'm in the park.

LUKE Tell you what, though. If our parents weren't …

MEGAN Shh!! Dad, say that again. What? The hospital? Mum?

4

DEVELOPING SPEAKING

2 Work in pairs. Discuss what happens next in the story. Write down your ideas.

Perhaps Megan has to go to the hospital.

3 ▶️ EP6 **Watch to find out how the story continues.**

4 Answer the questions.

1 What happened to Megan's mother?
2 When will her mother go home?
3 What is the problem for Megan's father?
4 Why can Megan help without going to school?
5 What does Megan say to the others is 'the good thing'?
6 What does Luke mean when he says: 'It's all ups and downs'?

PHRASES FOR FLUENCY

1 Find the expressions 1–6 in the story. Who says them? Match them to the definitions a–f.

1 I suppose so.   a What I want to say is …
2 I mean, …   b I really don't care.
3 Whatever.   c Here's what I think …
4 I can't wait.   d I think that's possibly true.
5 Wait and see.   e You'll know in the future.
6 Tell you what …   f I hope it happens very soon.

2 Complete the conversations. Use the expressions 1–6 in Exercise 1.

1 A I'm going to see the new Ryan Gosling film on Saturday! _____ !
  B _____ – we could go together. _____ , if that's OK with you.
2 A What are you going to give me for my birthday?
  B _____ . It's a surprise!
3 A You look so funny in that yelllow shirt.
  B _____ , Alex.
4 A Can I go out tonight, Dad?
  B _____ . But don't be late back, OK?

WordWise
Expressions with *do*

1 Complete the sentences from the video.
1 She was doing some _____ upstairs.
2 I can do the _____ and everything.
3 Thanks. She's doing _____ , though.

2 Complete the sentences with a word from the list.

ice cream | homework | cooking | well

1 Joe's upstairs – he's doing his _____ .
2 Did you do _____ in your exam?
3 They do great _____ at the new café.
4 Mum has a rest on Sundays and we all do the _____ .

3 SPEAKING **Complete the questions. Then ask and answer with a partner.**

1 _____ you _____ a lot of exercise?
2 Where _____ you _____ your homework?
3 _____ you _____ OK with your schoolwork these days?
4 Who _____ the cleaning in your house?

Workbook page 102

FUNCTIONS
Sympathising

1 Complete the extracts from the story with the phrases in the list.

Poor you. | That's a shame.
I'm sorry to hear that. | poor thing.

1 MEGAN   But I know one thing: he shouts at me all the time. Everything I do is wrong.
  OLIVIA   _____ .
2 MEGAN   Oh, _____ . Well, she'll be home tomorrow.
  DAD   That's right. Then a few days at home.
3 RYAN   _____ , Megan.
  OLIVIA   Me too.
  MEGAN   Thanks. She's doing OK, though.
4 MEGAN   But it means I can't go out with you guys on Friday.
  RYAN   _____ .

2 Read the situations. What can you say in each one?

1 You meet a friend. You know that your friend lost something important yesterday.

  Poor you!

2 You hear that Alex broke his arm last weekend. You meet Alex's brother.

3 Your neighbour says: 'I feel terrible today – I think I'm ill.'

A

B

C

READING

1 Match the words with the photos. Write 1–6 in the boxes.

1 bicycle | 2 bus | 3 boat | 4 car | 5 plane | 6 train

2 Name other kinds of transport in English.

3 SPEAKING Work in pairs. Ask and answer the questions.

How do you travel …
- to school?
- to the cinema?
- to the shops?
- when you go on holiday?

I usually go by bike.

Sometimes I take the bus. Sometimes I walk.

Sometimes I walk, but sometimes my dad drives.

4 SPEAKING Work in pairs or small groups. Read about these people. For each one, say how you think they could travel.

1 A British family – wife, husband and two children – want to go to the USA on holiday.

2 A student living in London wants to go to Paris.

3 A businesswoman who works in a city is going to a meeting on the other side of the city.

4 Three teenagers in a city want to go to a party at a house that is five kilometres away.

5 SPEAKING Think about the ways of travelling in Exercises 1 and 2. Which one(s) is (are):
- cheap?
- dangerous?
- expensive?
- boring?
- exciting?
- your favourite?
- an adventure?
- your least favourite?

E

D

F

6 Look at the photos and the title of the blog on page 111. What do you think the blog is about? Choose one of the following.

1 Someone who travels to many different places.

2 Different ways to travel.

3 Different places to travel to in the world.

7 ◄)) 2.38 Read and listen to the blog and check your ideas.

8 Read the blog again. Correct the information in these sentences.

1 Nora Dunn wanted to travel the world until she got old.

2 Nora gets her money from some rich friends.

3 Sometimes she writes home to ask for some money.

4 She does the same job everywhere she goes.

5 She travelled by boat to the Caribbean.

6 She has appeared on television in every country she's visited.

7 Life is always easy for her when she travels.

8 She has a website to tell people how to spend a lot of money travelling.

Ted's Travel Blog

HOME   ABOUT   NEWS   CONTACT

The non-stop traveller

Hello to all my readers. This week, I've decided to write about travel. Perhaps, like me, you've always thought that travelling is something for rich people. Well, now I think I've been wrong all this time. Why? Well, I've discovered Nora Dunn.

Nora is one of a new kind of traveller – a professional world traveller. She travels all the time. Nora is from Toronto, Canada and until she was 30, she had a business there. But then she made a big decision. Her dream was to travel the world – and to do it before she got old! So she sold her business and got rid of her belongings. And off she went.

Nora hasn't got rich parents or anyone who gives her money. And she doesn't have a high-paying job. But she's learned how to travel without spending lots of money.

Nora goes to a place and stays there for some time. She works to earn enough money to have a good time and to save a bit, then she moves on to another place. She prefers simple forms of transport like trains or buses, but of course there are times when planes are a necessity. And she writes from wherever she is, which earns her some money too. She's done a lot of different jobs, including working in hotels and in restaurants. And she's learned things like cooking and meditation.

So where has Nora been? Well, everywhere! She's been to all five continents and she's travelled to over thirty countries. All in six years! She's taken a train across Canada and she's travelled by train from Portugal to Vietnam – an incredible journey. She's lived on a boat in the Caribbean and she's worked for her accommodation in Hawaii, Australia, New Zealand, Spain, England, Grenada and Switzerland, and a number of other places too. And she's been on television shows in three countries. She's had a lot of fantastic adventures, and she hasn't stopped finding new things!

Some of her experiences have not been easy ones. In 2008 she helped people in Thailand and Burma after a cyclone hit their countries. And in 2009 she helped to fight forest fires in Australia.

So, she's seen a lot so far. She's learned that full-time travel doesn't have to be expensive, and she knows now that there are plenty of ways to do it – so many ways, in fact, that she's started a website to tell other people about them. It's theprofessionalhobo.com. I've seen lots of travel sites, and this is one of the best. Have a look. Perhaps you'll be the next 'world traveller'?

See you next week.

■ THiNK VALUES ■

Travel broadens the mind

1 **Read what people said about Nora Dunn. Match the comments 1–4 with the values a–d. Write a–d in the boxes.**

1 [ ] She's seen so many different countries, so I think she probably understands all kinds of people.

2 [ ] She's probably a better person now, because she's learned so many things.

3 [ ] I think it's wonderful, what she did in Burma with the cyclone and in Australia with the fire.

4 [ ] I think it's great that she's living her life without thinking about money all the time.

a helping other people
b self-improvement
c not worrying about money
d learning about other cultures

2 **SPEAKING** How important are the values in Exercise 1 for you? Put them in order from 1–4. Compare your ideas in class. Say why you think the values are important or not.

GRAMMAR
Present perfect simple

1 Complete the sentences from the blog on page 111. Then complete the rule.

1 Perhaps, like me, you _____ always _____ that travelling is something for rich people.

2 Now, I think I _____ wrong all this time.

3 She _____ a lot of different jobs.

4 So where _____ Nora _____ ?

5 Some of her experiences _____ easy ones.

> **RULE:** Use the present perfect to talk about actions that happened some time in your life up to now.
> Form the present perfect with the present simple form of _____ + past participle.

2 <u>Underline</u> other examples of the present perfect in the blog on page 111.

3 Complete the table.

Positive	Negative	Questions	Short answers
I/you/we/they 've (¹ _____) worked	I/you/we/they haven't (have not) worked	⁴ _____ I/you/we/they worked?	Yes, I/you/we/they ⁶ _____ . No, I/you/we/they haven't.
he/she/it 's (² _____) worked	he/she/it hasn't (³ _____) worked	⁵ _____ he/she/it worked?	Yes, he/she/it has. No, he/she/it ⁷ _____ .

4 Complete the past participles. Use the irregular verbs list on page 128 of the Workbook to help you.

base form	past participle	base form	past participle
0 be	*been*	6 speak	_____
1 do	_____	7 eat	_____
2 go	_____	8 take	_____
3 see	_____	9 fly	_____
4 write	_____	10 swim	_____
5 meet	_____	11 win	_____

> **LOOK!**
> 1 *She **has gone** to New York.* = She is not here now – she is in New York.
> 2 *She **has been** to New York.* = She went to New York and came back (at some time in the past).

5 Jack and Diane are 25 years old. When they were teenagers, they wanted to do many things – and they have done some of them but not all of them. Look at the table. Complete the sentences about them.

	learn French	visit Paris	write a book	work in the USA	make a lot of money
Diane	✓	✗	✓	✓	✗
Jack	✓	✓	✗	✗	✗

0 Jack and Diane *have learned* French.

1 Diane _____ Paris.

2 Diane _____ a book.

3 Jack _____ Paris.

4 Jack _____ in the USA.

5 They _____ a lot of money.

6 **WRITING** Look at the information about Sue and Harry. Write sentences about them.

	visit another country	fly in a plane	swim in the sea	touch a snake	take a driving test
Sue	✓	✗	✗	✗	✓
Harry	✓	✓	✗	✓	✗

7 **SPEAKING** Work in pairs. Say things about yourself and people you know.
Remember: don't say when in the past.

> *My mother has lived in Africa.*
> *I've won two tennis competitions.*

Workbook page 108 ➤

LISTENING

1 ◀)) 2.39 **Steve Anderson is at his old school giving a talk about his travels. Listen to the end of Steve's talk. Mark the statements T (true) or F (false).**

1 He wants to get married and start a family. ☐

2 When he was younger, he didn't like staying at home. ☐

3 He's going to stop travelling soon. ☐

2 ◀)) 2.40 **Now the children ask Steve questions. Listen and match the events with the places.**

1 ☐ The most interesting place he's been to.

2 ☐ The place where he ate a cooked spider.

3 ☐ The place where he was ill.

a Africa **b** India **c** Mexico

3 ◀)) 2.40 **Listen again and answer the questions.**

1 Has he ever eaten snake?

2 Did he like the spider that he ate?

3 Has he had any accidents in a minibus or taxi?

4 What do tourists and travellers take with them?

GRAMMAR
Present perfect with *ever* / *never*

1 **Complete the sentences with *ever* or *never* and complete the rule.**

1 I've _____ eaten snake.

2 Have you _____ eaten anything really horrible?

> **RULE:** When we use the present perfect to talk about experiences and we want to say:
> • 'at no time in (my) life' we use the word ¹_____
> • 'at any time in (your) life' we use the word ²_____
> The words *ever* and *never* usually come between *have* and the past participle.

2 **Complete the mini dialogues with the words in the list.**

been | yes | eaten | have
never | no | ever | played

1 A Have you _____ watched a silent film?
  B Yes, I _____ .

2 A Have you ever _____ to the Olympic games?
  B _____ , I've never been to them.

3 A Have you ever _____ tennis?
  B _____ , I have.

4 A Have you ever _____ a really hot curry?
  B No, I've _____ tried curry.

Workbook page 109

FUNCTIONS
Talking about life experiences

Work in pairs. Ask and answer the questions

1 ever / see / a snake?
2 ever / eat / something horrible?
3 ever / be / on television?
4 ever / speak / to someone from the USA?
5 ever / win / a prize?
6 ever / be / to another country?

> *Have you ever seen a snake?*
> *Yes I have. It was a python at the zoo.*
> *No, I haven't.*

SPEAKING

Work in pairs. Think of a famous person. Ask about things that the famous person has done in their life, and imagine the answers. Use some of the verbs in the list.

travel | stay | play | win | eat | see | drive | write

> *Mr President — have you ever eaten fried spiders?*
> *Yes, I have. I eat them all the time.*

■ TRAIN TO THiNK ■
Exploring differences

1 **SPEAKING** **Work in small groups. Look at the pairs of things. Answer the questions.**

a What is the same?
b What is different?

1 A car and a taxi
2 A train and a plane
3 A holiday and a journey
4 A tourist and a traveller

The same: a car and a taxi have wheels / doors / a driver.
Different: you drive your car but a taxi-driver drives the taxi. In a taxi, you have to pay.

2 **SPEAKING** **Compare your ideas with others in the class.**

> **Pronunciation**
> Sentence stress
> Go to page 121.

READING

1 Read the interview. Put the four questions in the correct places.

a Have you ever had any famous passengers?

b Have passengers ever left anything in your taxi?

c What's the worst part of your job?

d When did you start?

THE TAXI DRIVER

Fiona McIntyre is a taxi driver in London. She tells us about her work and some of her experiences.

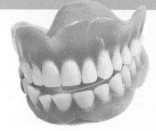

1 _____

I've been a taxi driver for about five years. Before that I was a bus driver in London, and I enjoyed it, but I wanted to be more independent so I changed and started driving my taxi.

2 _____

Oh yes. I've had film stars, politicians, you know, lots of famous people. About a year ago, a really famous actor got in my taxi. I took him to the airport. There was a lot of traffic and it took a long time to get there, so he missed his plane. It wasn't my fault but when he got out of the taxi, he said some things that weren't very polite! I said to him, 'Next time, take a bus!'

3 _____

Oh yes! People have left all kinds of things in here – a suitcase, a hat, mobile phones of course, even a dog once! Years ago, a woman left a pair of shoes on the back seat. And one time a passenger left his teeth here! Not real teeth, of course – false teeth.

And people have asked me to do some strange jobs. Once a doctor stopped me outside a hospital and asked me to take a skeleton to another hospital. And I did. But I asked the doctor to pay first – the skeleton couldn't pay, after all!

4 _____

Good question. I've always enjoyed being a taxi driver and I don't want to change. But of course, sometimes, it's not great. I don't like driving around without a passenger, but it's better than just waiting at the airport or at a railway station. I think that's the worst part – waiting.

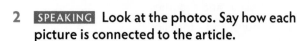

2 **SPEAKING** Look at the photos. Say how each picture is connected to the article.

> *There's a picture of a bus. She was a bus driver before she became a taxi driver.*

3 Read the interview again and answer the questions.

1 Why did she stop being a bus driver?

2 Why was the famous actor angry when he got out of the taxi?

3 Why did she ask the doctor to pay first when she took the skeleton?

4 What two things does she not like about her job?

4 **SPEAKING** Work in two groups. Group A: you are bus drivers. Group B: you are flight attendants. In your group, think of answers to these questions.

1 When did you start your job?

2 Tell us about an accident you've had.

3 Tell us about a funny moment you've had.

4 Do you like your job or do you want to change?

5 **SPEAKING** Work in pairs – one student from Group A with one student from Group B. Ask and answer the questions.

6 **SPEAKING** Decide whose answers were best: the bus driver's or the flight attendant's.

GRAMMAR
Present perfect vs. past simple

1 **Complete the things Fiona said in the article on page 114. Complete the rule with the names of the tenses.**

1 I _____ film stars, politicians, you know, lots of famous people.

2 A year ago, a really famous actor _____ in my taxi.

3 People _____ all kinds of things.

4 One time, a passenger _____ a pair of false teeth.

5 People _____ me to do some strange jobs.

6 Once, a doctor _____ me outside a hospital and _____ me to take a skeleton to another hospital.

> **RULE:** Use the ¹_____ to talk about situations or actions at a particular time in the past.
>
> Use the ²_____ to talk about situationsor actions in the past, when we don't say when they happened.

2 **Find more examples of verbs in the past simple and present perfect in the article on page 114.**

3 (Circle) **the correct forms.**

My name's Michael Edwards and I'm 26. ¹*I've been / I was* very lucky in my life because I have a good job and I travel a lot for work. ²*I've lived / I lived* in three different countries: Thailand, India and Singapore. ³*I've lived / I lived* in Singapore from 2012 to 2014. I live in Thailand now.

⁴*I've got / I got* married two years ago. My wife and I travel a lot together and ⁵*we've seen / we saw* some wonderful places. Last year ⁶*we've seen / we saw* the Taj Mahal in India.

⁷*I've done / I did* some crazy things in my life but the craziest was last month – ⁸*I've gone / I went* by minibus all the way to the north of Thailand. ⁹*It's been / It was* really scary!

Workbook page 109 ➤

VOCABULARY
Transport and travel

1 🔊2.43 **Write the words under the photos. Listen and check.**

~~a minibus~~ | a helicopter | a tram | a motorbike a scooter | an underground train

0 _a minibus_

1 _____

2 _____

3 _____

4 _____

5 _____

Travel verbs

2 **Complete the sentences with the correct form of the verbs in the list.**

~~miss~~ | fly | catch | take | ride | drive

0 I had to walk home because I _missed_ the bus.

1 I ran very fast but I didn't _____ the train.

2 I have never _____ in a helicopter.

3 My brother's got a motorbike and now he's learning to _____ it.

4 We got in the car and we _____ to France.

5 The rain was terrible so we _____ a taxi.

3 **SPEAKING** **Work in pairs. Ask each other questions. Use the verbs in Exercise 2 and the forms of transport you can see on this page and page 110.**

> *Have you ever flown in a helicopter?*

> *No, I haven't. Have you ever taken a tram?*

> *Yes, I took a tram in Lisbon when I was on holiday.*

Workbook page 110 ➤

Culture

1 Look at the photos and answer the questions. Then say what you think the article is going to be about.

Where can you see
- a student riding to school on a donkey?
- children walking to school along some rail tracks?

2 ◀))2.44 Read and listen to the article and say which country each photo is from.

Hard journeys for schoolchildren

'How do you get to school?' This question often gets an answer like 'By bus' or 'I walk' or 'My parents take me by car'. But not always – there are children in many different parts of the world who, every day, have to go on a difficult journey in order to get to their lessons. They travel for kilometres on foot, or by boat, bicycle, donkey or train. They cross deserts, mountains, rivers, snow and ice: for example, the children of the Iñupiat community in Alaska go to school and then come back when it is dark, in extremely cold temperatures. And they are not the only ones – kids in many countries do this and more.

These children in Indonesia have to cross a bridge ten metres above a dangerous river to get to their class on time . (The bridge fell down in 2001 after very heavy rain.) Then they walk many more kilometres through the forest to their school in Banten village.

A pupil at Gulu Village Primary School, China, rides a donkey as his grandfather walks beside him. Gulu is a mountain village in a national park. The school is far away from the village. It is halfway up a mountain, so it takes five hours to climb from the bottom of the mountain to the school. The children have a dangerous journey: the path is only 45 centimetres wide in some places.

A

In Sri Lanka, some children have to cross a piece of wood between two walls of an old castle every morning. Their teacher watches them carefully. But in Sri Lanka, many girls don't go to school – they have to go to work or get married young. So girls are happy to take a risk in order to get to school.

Six-year old Fabricio Oliveira gets on his donkey every morning to ride with his friends for over an hour through a desert region in the very dry Sertão area of north-east Brazil. Their school is in Extrema. It's a tiny village – only very few people live there.

B

These children live in poor houses on Chetla Road in Delhi, India. Their homes are near the busy and dangerous railway lines that go to Alipur station. Every morning they walk along the tracks to get to their school, forty minutes away.

So one question we can ask is: why do the children do this? Because their parents make them do it? The answer, in many cases, is no – it's because for them going to school means a better future: They hope to get a job and money, so they can help their families and their neighbours . And this is why rivers, deserts or danger won't stop them on their way to school.

C

3 **Read the article again. What difficulties do children in these places face to get to school?**

1 The children of the Iñupiat community in Alaska.

2 The children who go to the school in Banten, Indonesia.

3 The children who go to the Gulu Village Primary School, China.

4 The children who go to school in Galle, Sri Lanka.

5 Fabricio Oliveira in Brazil.

6 The children who live along The Chetla Road in Delhi, India.

4 VOCABULARY **There are eight highlighted words in the article. Match the words with these meanings. Write the words.**

0	from one side to the other	*wide*
1	people living in houses near you	_____
2	a trip	_____
3	do something that can be dangerous	_____
4	a group of houses usually in the countryside	_____
5	the things that trains move on	_____
6	very, very small	_____
7	not late	_____

5 SPEAKING **Which journey is the one you would least like to have to do? Compare with others in the class.**

WRITING
Someone I admire

1 **Read Mariana's essay about 'Someone I admire'. Answer the questions.**

1 When and where was her uncle Tim born?

2 Where does he live now, and when did he move there?

3 How does he travel in his work?

4 What does he want to do in the future?

5 Why does Mariana admire her uncle?

2 **Find examples in the essay of the word *in* with these things.**

1	a year	3	a city
2	a month	4	a country

3 **Look at the four paragraphs of Mariana's essay about her uncle. Match the paragraphs with the contents.**

Paragraph 1	a	What he does, and how
Paragraph 2	b	Why she admires him
Paragraph 3	c	When and where he was born
Paragraph 4	d	Why he does these things

Someone I admire

(1) My uncle Tim is a really great guy. He was born in England in 1980, in a city called Halifax, but now he lives and works in Cambodia. He went to Cambodia in 2014.

(2) My uncle is a doctor and he worked at a hospital in Manchester for a few years. But in 2014 he decided to go and work in small villages in Cambodia because he heard that they needed doctors. He travels from village to village to help people. He has a small motorbike that he uses. Sometimes, though, he goes in a very small plane because the roads aren't good enough.

(3) Uncle Tim says that he wants to stay there because there is a lot of work to do. He has also met a girl there – he told me in an email that they are getting married in July next year. Uncle Tim hopes that he can help to teach Cambodian people to become doctors in the future. He has learned a lot of the language – that can't be easy!

(4) I said before that he's a great guy. Why do I think that? Well, because he is helping other people and is happy doing that, and because he has learned a lot about another culture.

4 **Think of someone that you admire: a famous person; or someone you know in your own life; or someone you invent.**

For the person, think about:

* facts about their life (when they were born, etc.)
* what they do, where and how, when they started
* what they want to do in the future
* why you admire them

5 **Write an essay called 'Someone I admire' in about 150 words. Use the example essay and language above to help you.**

READING AND WRITING
Part 5: Multiple-choice cloze

1 **Read the travel blog. Choose the best word (A, B or C) for each space.**

I love **(0)** _travelling_ . I spend all my holidays visiting other countries. I never stay at home. So far I've **(1)**_____ to 56 different countries and this year, if I **(2)**_____ the money, I'll visit three more: Cambodia, Vietnam and Laos. It's a part of Asia I've **(3)**_____ been to so I'm really excited about this trip. I want to make the whole journey without **(4)**_____ a plane. I plan to get to Thailand by boat and then **(5)**_____ buses to visit these countries. On the way home, I'll travel **(6)**_____ train through China and India, and then through Europe. It **(7)**_____ be a short trip – it **(8)**_____ probably take about four months. I hope my boss doesn't mind me taking some time off work!

0	(A) travelling	B	travel	C	to travelling
1	A gone	B	been	C	went
2	A had	B	will have	C	have
3	A ever	B	always	C	never
4	A taking	B	riding	C	going
5	A travel	B	miss	C	take
6	A on	B	by	C	in
7	A isn't	B	won't	C	will
8	A will	B	is	C	can

Part 8: Information transfer　Workbook page 107 ➤

2 **Read the information about the school trip. Complete Gina's notes.**

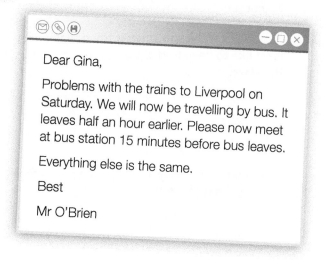

Dear Gina,

Problems with the trains to Liverpool on Saturday. We will now be travelling by bus. It leaves half an hour earlier. Please now meet at bus station 15 minutes before bus leaves.

Everything else is the same.

Best

Mr O'Brien

School trip to the Tate Art Museum
Liverpool
Date [1]_____
Travelling by [2]_____
Transport leaves at [3]_____
Meet at the [4]_____ about 9.30 am
Cost [5]£ [1]_____

LISTENING
Part 2: Matching

3 🔊2.45 **Listen to Jack talking to a friend about his transport project. How does each person get to school? For questions 1–5, write a letter (A–H) next to each person.**

0	Jack	F	A	bike
1	Olivia		B	boat
2	Rashid		C	taxi
3	Morris		D	bus
4	Leslie		E	car
5	Adam		F	on foot
			G	scooter
			H	train

VOCABULARY

1 **Complete the sentences with the words in the list. There are two extra words.**

neck | trams | ride | scooter | helicopter | tongue | caught | back | stomach ache | missed | lip | flew

1 He's really rich. He goes to work by _____ and he lands on the roof of his office building.
2 I've got a _____ . I think it was something I ate.
3 We _____ the last train home and so we slept in the station.
4 Open your mouth. I want to take a look at your _____ .
5 I can't _____ a motorbike and I don't want to learn how to. I think they're dangerous.
6 I fell and cut my mouth and made my top _____ bleed.
7 My dad rides his _____ to work. It's quicker than going by car and a lot cheaper.
8 We _____ over the mountains in a small plane. The views were fantastic!
9 I always sleep on my _____ .
10 Many cities are now using _____ to get people to and from work.

/10

GRAMMAR

2 **Put the words in order to make sentences.**

1 phone / I'll / home / you / get / soon / as / I / as
2 taxi / I / train, / miss / If / the / take / a / I'll
3 ever / Have / Europe / you / been / to / ?
4 seen / She's / sea / never / the
5 different / five / lived / countries / in / They've
6 grandchildren / be / easy / for / won't / our / Life

3 **Find and correct the mistake in each sentence.**

1 She's played football yesterday.
2 If we will be late, the teacher will be angry.
3 I have ever broken an arm or a leg.
4 I've never gone to America.
5 She has took a lot of photos on holiday.
6 One day in the future people will living on the moon.

/12

FUNCTIONAL LANGUAGE

4 **Write the missing words.**

1 A What's the _____ ?
  B My leg _____ a lot.
2 A I've _____ a headache.
  B I'm sorry to _____ that. Can I get you an aspirin?
3 A Have you _____ been to Canada?
  B No, I _____ .
4 A Do you think it _____ rain tomorrow?
  B I don't know. I'm not _____ .

/8

MY SCORE /30

| 22 – 30 |
| 10 – 21 |
| 0 – 9 |

119

PRONUNCIATION

UNIT 7
Vowel sounds: /ʊ/ and /uː/

1 🔊 **2.08** **Listen to the dialogue.**

LUKE   Let's look in this room, Sue.

SUE   Wow! It's got things from the moon in it.

LUKE   Look at these cool boots! I saw them in our science book.

SUE   We should take a photo for our school project, Luke.

2 Say the words with the short /ʊ/ vowel sound. Then say the words with the long /uː/ vowel sound.

3 🔊 **2.09** Listen and repeat. Then practise with a partner.

UNIT 8
Strong and weak forms of *was* and *were*

1 🔊 **2.13** **Listen to the dialogue.**

GIRL   Was she shopping?

BOY   Yes, she was. She was shopping for socks.

GIRL   Were they doing their homework?

BOY   No, they weren't. They were learning to surf!

2 Say the words with the /ɒ/ sound. Now say the words with the /ɜː/ sound. When *was* and *were* aren't stressed, we use the /ə/ sound. It's the same as /ɜː/ but shorter.

3 🔊 **2.14** Listen and repeat. Then practise with a partner.

UNIT 9
Vowel sounds: /ɪ/ and /aɪ/

1 🔊 **2.21** **Listen to the dialogue.**

JILL   I'd like to live in the wild. What about you, Mike?

MIKE   I prefer a city lifestyle. I don't like lions or tigers – or insects!

JILL   But living in the wild's much more exciting!

MIKE   Yes, Jill – and it's more frightening, too.

2 Say the words with the short /ɪ/ vowel sound. Then say the words with the long /aɪ/ vowel sound.

3 🔊 **2.22** Listen and repeat. Then practise with a partner.

UNIT 10
Voiced /ð/ and unvoiced /θ/ consonants

1 🔊 **2.27** **Listen to the dialogue.**

BETH   Look – there's the theatre.

HARRY   That's not the right one, Beth.

BETH   Well, it says, 'The Fifth Avenue Theatre'.

HARRY   But we want the one on Third Street!

2 Say the words with the voiced /ð/. Then say the words with the unvoiced /θ/.

3 🔊 **2.28** Listen and repeat. Then practise with a partner.

UNIT 11
The /h/ consonant sound

1 🔊 **2.32** **Listen to the dialogue.**

DR HARRIS   Who's next? Oh, hello Harry. How can I help you?

HARRY   Well, Dr Harris – my head's very hot!

DR HARRIS   Let me see ... does it hurt here?

HARRY   Yes, doctor! That feels horrible!

DR HARRIS   It's your hat, Harry. It's too small!

2 Say the words starting with the /h/ consonant sound.

3 🔊 **2.33** Listen and repeat. Then practise with a partner.

UNIT 12
Sentence stress

1 🔊 **2.41** **Listen to the stress in these sentences.**

<u>Car</u> – <u>plane</u> – <u>bike</u> – <u>train</u>.
A <u>car</u>, a <u>plane</u>, a <u>bike</u>, a <u>train</u>.
A <u>car</u> and a <u>plane</u> and a <u>bike</u> and a <u>train</u>.
A <u>car</u> and then a <u>plane</u> and then a <u>bike</u> and then a <u>train</u>.

2 Which words are stressed in every sentence? What happens to the other words?

3 🔊 **2.42** Listen and repeat. Then practise with a partner.

UNIT 7
have to / don't have to

We always use the base form of the verb after *have to / don't have to.*

✓ He **has to tidy** his room today.
✗ He has to ~~tidied~~ his room today.
✗ He has to ~~tidying~~ his room today.

We use the correct form of *do + not/n't + have to* to say that something isn't necessary. We don't use *haven't to.*

✓ You **don't have to help** me. I can do it.
✗ You ~~haven't to~~ help me. I can do it.

Find six mistakes. Correct them.

I have to do a lot of housework at home, but I'm OK about that. I have to tidying my room, but I haven't to vacuum the floor. My brother has to does that. We have to do the washing up, but we don't have do the washing. My dad does that once a week. I haven't to do the cooking – my mum likes cooking. She says it helps her to relax. Of course, I have to doing my homework every day after school. I'm not OK about that!

UNIT 8
Past continuous vs. past simple

We use the past continuous to talk about background actions in the past, and the past simple for actions which happened at one moment in the past.

✓ I **was watching** television when the lights **went** out.
✗ I ~~watched~~ television when the lights went out.

Complete the story with the past continuous or past simple of the verb in brackets.

The surprise!

It ¹_____ (happen) last Saturday while I ²_____ (have) a party at my house. At 9 o'clock, we ³_____ (dance) and having a fantastic time. Then, suddenly, the lights ⁴_____ (go) out. I ⁵_____ (close) my eyes and screamed! But when I ⁶_____ (stop), I heard that all my friends ⁷_____ (laugh). When I ⁸_____ (open) my eyes, everybody was smiling at me. When my mum ⁹_____ (arrive) with a cake and candles, I finally understood …

UNIT 9
Comparative adjectives

We use *more* + adjective with two syllables or more to form the comparative. We don't use *more* with adjectives with one syllable or with adjectives that are already in the comparative form (e.g. *smaller, colder, friendlier*).

✓ His room is **smaller** than mine.
✗ His room is ~~more small~~ than mine.
✗ His room is ~~more smaller~~ than mine.

<u>Underline</u> the correct sentence.

1 a Lions can run more faster during the night.
  b Lions can run faster during the night.
2 a The weather in the Kalahari is drier than in Europe.
  b The weather in the Kalahari is more dry than in Europe.
3 a It's more hotter in the summer than in the winter.
  b It's hotter in the summer than in the winter.
4 a People in the countryside are friendlier than people in the city.
  b People in the countryside are more friendlier than people in the city.

can / can't for ability

We always use the base form of the verb after *can / can't.*

✓ He **can swim**, but he **can't surf**.
✗ He can ~~swam~~, but he can't ~~to surf~~.

(Circle) the correct verb form.

1 I love living by the sea. On sunny days, I can *went / going / go* to the beach.
2 On cold days, you can *do / doing / to do* the shopping in the town centre.
3 We can *learning / learn / to learn* a lot about wildlife from nature programmes.
4 You can't *drive / driving / drove* a car if you're fifteen.
5 They can't **to** *come / coming / come* to the party because they're on holiday.

UNIT 10
be going to for intentions

> We use the present tense of *be* + *going to* + base form of the verb to talk about our intentions in the future. Remember to use the present tense of *be*.
>
> ✓ He **is going to study** all weekend.
> ✗ He ~~going~~ to study all weekend.

Complete the sentences with *be going to* and the verb in brackets.

1 He _____ (paint) his bedroom on Saturday.
2 I've bought a new chair. I _____ (put) it near the TV.
3 We _____ (visit) my cousin because he is ill.
4 They _____ (go) to the sports centre by car.
5 We _____ (watch) a film tonight.

Present continuous for arrangements

> We use the present continuous to talk about arrangements for the future. We don't use the present simple.
>
> ✓ I'm **going to visit** my grandparents tomorrow.
> ✗ I ~~go~~ to visit my grandparents tomorrow.

> To ask questions about arrangements, we use question word + *be* + subject + the *-ing* form of the verb. Remember to put the words in the correct order.
>
> ✓ What **are you doing** tomorrow?
> ✗ What ~~you are doing~~ tomorrow?

Find six mistakes in the dialogue. Correct them.

LARA   Hi Sam, what you are doing on Saturday?

SAM   Well, in the morning, I play football in the park.

LARA   What are you doing in the afternoon?

SAM   I don't do anything. What are you doing?

LARA   I paint my bedroom.

SAM   Cool! What colour do you use?

LARA   I'm going to choose the colour when I go to the shop.

SAM   Which shop are you going to?

LARA   I go to the shop in the high street at 2 o'clock.

SAM   OK. I'll meet you there! I can help you to choose.

UNIT 11
will / won't for future predictions

> We use the present continuous to talk about things happening now and future arrangements. We use *will* or *won't* + base form to make future predictions.
>
> ✓ I'm sure you**'ll do** well in your test next week.
> ✗ I'm sure you ~~are doing~~ well in your test next week.
> ✓ I'm **going** to a party on Saturday.
> ✗ I ~~will go~~ to a party on Saturday.

Choose present continuous or *'ll / won't* to complete the email.

To: gareth@email.co.uk
Subject: Holiday!

Hi Gareth,

I don't think [1]*I'll see / I'm seeing* you before my holiday. [2]*We'll leave / We're leaving* on Saturday, so [3]*I'm being / I'll be* very busy. [4]*I'll go / I'm going* shopping on Friday, so [5]*I'm not being / I won't be* at art class. [6]*I'll need / I'm needing* to buy some shorts – my dad says [7]*it'll be / it's being* really hot in Tunisia! [8]*I'll phone / I'm phoning* you on Friday night if I have time. I have to go now. [9]*I'll help / I'm helping* my sister with her homework.

Marcus

UNIT 12
Present perfect simple

> We use the present perfect simple to talk about situations or actions that happened some time in the past.
>
> ✓ I **have met** a lot of famous actors.
> ✗ I ~~met~~ a lot of famous actors.

> We use the past simple to talk about situations or actions at a specific time in the past.
>
> ✓ A year ago, I **met** a famous actor.
> ✗ A year ago, I ~~have met~~ a famous actor.

Find seven mistakes in the text. Correct them.

My parents work for international companies, so I travelled a lot. I've lived in Europe, Asia and the USA. Two years ago, I have lived in Spain for six months. My brother's only three, so he only went to Europe and he forgot that trip! My dad travelled to more places. He has been to Australia and New Zealand last year, but we never visited England.

STUDENT A

UNIT 7, PAGE 73

Student A

You are a son or daughter. You are at home.
You want to see a friend.

You are phoning your mum or dad about it.

When your mum/dad tells you that you should do some housework, ask her/him what you have to do.

Also, tell your mum/dad that there are some things she/he shouldn't forget. When she/he asks you what things, say:

She/He …

- should do the shopping
- shouldn't be late tonight (you want to watch a DVD together with her/him)
- mustn't forget to bring some chocolate biscuits!

The line is not very good so you have to ask your mum or dad several times to repeat what she/he has said.

UNIT 11, PAGE 107

Student A

Ask your questions and answer Student B's.

1 What will you do if it rains this weekend?
2 What will you do if the weather's nice?
3 How will you feel if your teacher gives you a lot of homework today?
4 What will you wear if you go out to a party this evening?
5 What film will you see if you go to the cinema this week?
6 What programme will you watch if you watch TV this evening?

STUDENT B

UNIT 7, PAGE 73

Student B

You are a mum or dad. Your son/daughter is phoning you.

Make sure he/she knows that he/she has to do some housework before he/she can go out. When he/she asks you, say:

He/She …

- has to tidy up his/her room
- should load the dishwasher
- mustn't forget to vacuum the floor

When your son or daughter tells you that there are things you shouldn't forget, ask them what things.

The line is not very good so you have to ask your son or daughter several times to repeat what he/she has said.

UNIT 11, PAGE 107

Student B

Ask your questions and answer Student A's.

1 What will you do if you stay at home this weekend?
2 What will you study if you go to university?
3 What will you buy if you go shopping this weekend?
4 How will you feel if your parents ask you to do a lot of housework this evening?
5 What video game will you play if you decide to play video games this evening?
6 Where will you go if you meet your friends tonight?

Acknowledgements

The authors and publishers acknowledge the following sources of copyright material and are grateful for the permissions granted. While every effort has been made, it has not always been possible to identify the sources of all the material used, or to trace all copyright holders. If any omissions are brought to our notice, we will be happy to include the appropriate acknowledgements on reprinting.

The publishers are grateful to the following for permission to reproduce copyright photographs and material:

T = Top, B = Below, L = Left, R = Right, C = Centre, B/G = Background

p. 66 (a): ©Evgeny Karandaev/iStock/360/Getty Images; p. 66 (b): ©f9photos/Shutterstock; p. 66 (c): ©Raywoo/iStock/360/Getty Images; p. 66 (d): ©Bart_Kowski/iStock/360/Getty Images; p. 66 (e): ©Oleksiy Mark/iStock/360/Getty Images; p. 66 (f): ©GeorgeMPhotography/Shutterstock; p. 67 (T): ©Frans Lemmens/Fuse/Getty Images; p. 67 (B): ©PhotoAlto/John Dowland/PhotoAlto Agency RF Collections/Getty Images; p. 68 (a): ©Lesia Sherstiuchenko/iStock/360/Getty Images; p. 68 (b, j): ©ppart/iStock/360/Getty Images; p. 68 (c): ©czekma13/iStock/360/Getty Images; p. 68 (d): ©Bet_Noire/iStock/360/Getty Images; p. 68 (e): ©Adrian Matthiassen/iStock/360/Getty Images; p. 68 (f): ©Evgeny Karandaev/iStock/360/Getty Images; p. 68 (g): ©cheyennezj/Shutterstock; p. 68 (h): ©arnau2098/iStock/360/Getty Images; p. 68 (i): ©aodaodaod/iStock/360/Getty Images; p. 71 (a): ©DragonImages/iStock/360/Getty Images; p. 71 (b): ©moodboard/Superstock; p. 71 (c): ©Roy Morsch/Corbis; p. 71 (d): ©Peter Dazeley/The Image Bank/Getty Images; p. 71 (e): ©Marjan Veljanoski/iStock/360/Getty Images; p. 71 (f): ©BananaStock/360/Getty Images; p. 71 (g): ©Anthony Hatley/Alamy; p. 71 (h): ©Fancy Collection/Fancy Collection/Superstock; p. 71 (i): ©woolzian/iStock/360/Getty Images; p. 71 (j): ©Margo Silver/The Image Bank/Getty Images; p. 74 (a): ©LuckyBusiness/iStock/360/Getty Images; p. 74 (b): ©Hugh Routledge/REX; p. 74 (c): ©Harry How/Getty Images Sport/Getty Images; p. 74 (d): ©LeeAnnWhite/iStock/360/Getty Images; p. 74 (e): ©Wallis/Photri Images/Alamy; p. 74 (f): ©mezzotint/Shutterstock; p. 75 (TL): ©PASCAL PAVANI/AFP/Getty Images; p. 75 (BR): ©Dujmovits, Ralf/National Geographic/Getty Images; p. 76 (a): ©Sport Picture Library/Alamy; p. 76 (b): ©Greg Epperson/iStock/360/Getty Images; p. 76 (c): ©Kzenon/Shutterstock; p. 76 (d): ©saintho/iStock/360/Getty Images; p. 76 (e): ©Jupiterimages/Stockbyte/Getty Images; p. 76 (f): ©Echo/Cultura/Getty Images; p. 77 (g): ©Ingram Publishing/Getty Images; p. 77 (h): ©Andrew Jalbert/iStock/360/Getty Images; p. 77 (i): ©Konstantin Shishkin/iStock/360/Getty Images; p. 77 (j): ©The Washington Post/Getty Images; p. 80 (L): ©The Print Collector/HIP/TopFoto; p. 80 (C, R): ©AFP/Getty Images; p. 81: ©Dennis Grombkowski/Getty Images Sport/Getty Images; p. 84: ©Design Pics/Keith Levit/Getty Images; p. 85 (TL): ©Dave Hamman/Gallo Images/Getty Images; p. 85 (TC): ©Nico Smit/iStock/360/Getty Images; p. 85 (TR): © Robert Harding World Imagery / Alamy; p. 85 (BL): © Steve Bloom Images / Alamy; p. 85 (BR): ©Eric VANDEVILLE/Gamma-Rapho via Getty Images; p. 87 (TL): ©USO/iStock/360/Getty Images; p. 87 (TR): ©PicturesWild/Shutterstock; p. 87 (BL): ©Johan Swanepoel/Shutterstock; p. 87 (BR): ©JOY TESSMAN/National Geographic/Getty Images; p. 88 (TL): ©fotografiche/iStock/360/Getty Images; p. 88 (TR): ©sprokop/iStock/360/Getty Images; p. 88 (BL): ©Evgeny Kovalev spb/Shutterstock; p. 91 (TL): ©Dragon Images/Shutterstock; p. 91 (TR): ©ep property/Alamy; p. 91 (B): ©Chimpinski/Shutterstock; p. 92 (TR): ©James MacKenzie, http://jamesmackenziephoto.com; p. 92 (L): ©Anastasios71/Shutterstock; p. 92 (BR): ©Kelly Cheng Travel Photography/Moment Open/Getty Images; p. 93 (T): ©Filip Fuxa/Alamy; p. 93 (B): ©NaturePL/Superstock; p. 96 (a): ©Alex Segre/Alamy; p. 96 (b): ©Terry Mathews/Alamy; p. 96 (c): ©Photofusion/REX; p. 96 (d): ©Christian Müller/iStock/360/Getty Images; p. 98 (TR): ©kevinhung/Shutterstock; p. 98 (BL): ©Sophele/iStock/360/Getty Images; p. 98 (BR): ©DON EMMERT/AFP/Getty Images; p. 99: ©Edward Westmacott/iStock/360/Getty Images; p. 100 (BL): ©Dark_Eni/iStock/360/Getty Images; p. 103 (TR): ©argus/Shutterstock; p. 103 (BL): ©kentoh/Shutterstock; p. 104 (a): ©malyugin/iStock/360/Getty Images; p. 104 (b): ©auremar/Shutterstock; p. 104 (c): ©Dudarev Mikhail/Shutterstock; p. 104 (d, h): ©AntonioGuillem/iStock/360/Getty Images; p. 104 (e): ©Hlib Shabashnyi/iStock/360/Getty Images; p. 104 (f): ©Halfpoint/Shutterstock; p. 104 (g): ©Voyagerix/Shutterstock; p. 104 (i): ©Marco Prati/Shutterstock; p. 104 (j): ©Viktor_Gladkov/iStock/360/Getty Images; p. 105 (L): ©Photographee.eu/Shutterstock; p. 105 (CL): ©Dora Zett/Shutterstock; p. 105 (CR): ©ATIC12/iStock/360/Getty Images; p. 105 (R): ©Thomas Lammeyer/Herma/360/Getty Images; p. 110 (a): ©hxdyl/iStock/360/Getty Images; p. 110 (b): ©Maremagnum/Photolibrary/Getty Images; p. 110 (c): ©Kimberly Brotherman/Moment Open/Getty Images; p. 110 (d): ©Felix Behnke/Collection Mix: Subjects/Getty Images; p. 110 (e): ©Dudarev Mikhail/Shutterstock; p. 110 (f): ©Marin Tomas/iStock/360/Getty Images; p. 111 (TL): ©Nora Dunn, aka The Professional Hobo, author of How to Get Free Accommodation Around the World. http://www.theprofessionalhobo.com/travel-tips-resources/get-free-accommodation-around-world/; p. 111 (CR): ©Oleg Kozlov/iStock/360/Getty Images; p. 111 (B): ©Robert Harding Picture Library/SuperStock; p. 114 (TL): ©Jupiterimages/Photos.com/360/Getty Images; p. 114 (TC): ©fotolibor/Shutterstock; p. 114 (TR): ©claudiodivizia/iStock/360/Getty Images; p. 114 (BL): ©Tim Ayers/Alamy; p. 114 (BR): ©abidal/iStock/360/Getty Images; p. 115 (TL): ©Charles O. Cecil/Alamy; p. 115 (TC): ©Matthew Grant/iStock/360/Getty Images; p. 115 (TR): ©gunnargren/iStock/360/Getty Images; p. 115 (BL): ©JackF/iStock/360/Getty Images; p. 115 (BC): ©KatPaws/iStock/360/Getty Images; p. 115 (BR): ©Onoky/Supertsock; p. 116 (a): ©AFP PHOTO/ANTARA/ASEP FATHULRAHMAN/Getty Images; p. 116 (b): ©Sipa Press/REX; p. 116 (c): ©ALFRED/SIPA/REX; p. 117: ©Echo/Cultura/Getty Images.

Commissioned photography by: Jon Barlow p 72, 90, 108.

Cover photographs by: : (L): ©Yuliya Koldovska/Shutterstock; (TR): ©Tim Gainey/Alamy; (BR): ©Oliver Burston/Alamy.

The publishers are grateful to the following illustrators: Maurizio De Angelis (Beehive Illustration) 102; David Semple 68, 104, 106, 112; Bryan Beach (Advocate Art) 86, 94, 111; Seb Camagajevac (Beehive Illustration) 69, 105; Anita Romeo (Advocate Art) 70; Arpad Olbey (Beehive Illustration) 78; Graham Kennedy 103

The publishers are grateful to the following contributors: Blooberry: text design and layouts; Claire Parson: cover design; Hilary Fletcher: picture research; Leon Chambers: audio recordings; Silversun Media Group: video production; Karen Elliott: Pronunciation sections; Diane Nicholls: Get it right! section

This page is intentionally left blank.

THiNK

WORKBOOK 1

A2

Herbert Puchta, Jeff Stranks & Peter Lewis-Jones

CAMBRIDGE
UNIVERSITY PRESS

This page is intentionally left blank.

CONTENTS

7 THE EASY LIFE

GRAMMAR

have to / don't have to SB p.68

1 ★☆☆ **Match the sentences with the signs.**

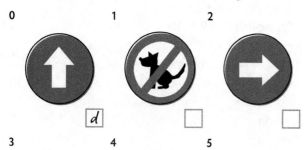

a You don't have to go to terminal A for flights to Paris.

b You have to wash your hands.

c Drivers have to turn right here.

d You have to go straight ahead.

e You have to leave your dog outside.

f Children don't have to pay.

2 ★★☆ **Write the sentences.**

0 the / a lot / have / we / Maths / study / test / to / for
We have to study a lot for the Maths test.

1 be / to / to / creative/ have / find / answer / We / the

_____

2 Sundays / make / to / has / he / On / breakfast

_____

3 early / you / get / have / Do / to / up / ?

_____

4 Lucas / school / tomorrow / have / doesn't / to / to / go

_____

5 have / I / phone / Do / to / you / ?

_____

6 me / to / You / have / help / don't

_____

3 ★★☆ **Match the questions and answers.**

0 Does your dad have to travel a lot in his job? `d`

1 Can I come to your place tomorrow? ☐

2 Why can't Susan come with us to the beach? ☐

3 Does your brother live in the city centre? ☐

4 Can I go to the match on Sunday? ☐

5 Why can't I go to the cinema tonight? ☐

a I spoke to her dad. She has to help at home.

b No, he doesn't. He has to take a train every day.

c I'm afraid you can't. We have to visit Grandma.

d Yes. He goes to other countries quite a lot.

e Because you have to tidy up your room.

f I'm sorry. You have to study for school. But why don't you go tomorrow?

4 ★★★ **Answer the questions so they are true for you.**

1 Do you have to get up early on weekdays?

_____

2 Do you have to use the Internet for your school work?

_____

3 Does your best friend have to help at home a lot?

_____

4 Do you have to do homework over the weekend?

_____

should / shouldn't SB p.69

5 ★☆☆ **Circle the correct words.**

0 The film starts in 10 minutes. We're late, so we *should* / shouldn't hurry up.

1 Dad doesn't know when he'll be home and says we *should / shouldn't* wait for him to eat.

2 It's just a T-shirt. Why does it cost £65? It *should / shouldn't* be so expensive.

3 Why are you angry with me? You *should / shouldn't* try to understand me.

4 She's on holiday until Monday. We *should / shouldn't* phone her before then.

5 Jane doesn't like her school uniform. She thinks students *should / shouldn't* wear what they want.

6 ★★☆ Complete the conversations. Use *should* or *shouldn't* and a phrase from the list.

~~put on a jumper~~ | stay much longer | talk to her
worry so much | leave home earlier

0 A I'm feeling cold.

   B I think you *should put on a jumper* .

1 A I can't believe it. I'm late for school again!

   B Perhaps you _____ .

2 A I don't think Jane is very happy at all.

   B Maybe you _____ .

3 A I'm a bit nervous about my English test.

   B You _____ . It's not helpful.

4 A It's getting late.

   B Yes, I know. We _____ .

7 ★★★ Answer the questions. Your answers can be funny or serious. Give reasons.

0 Should children get money for helping at home?

   Yes, they should because parents get money
   for their work too.

1 Should students get money for going to school?

   _____

2 Should the Internet be free for everybody?

   _____

3 Should every child have a tablet?

   _____

mustn't / don't have to SB p.70

8 ★☆☆ Look at the rules for a youth hostel. Circle the correct words in the sentences.

HOSTEL HOUSE RULES
- Last time for check out: 11.30 am.
- Music? OK, but use headphones.
- Switch off lights at 10 pm!
- Breakfast 7.30 – 9.30 am.
- Please wash up after eating.
- Don't walk into the bedrooms with your shoes on.

0 You *mustn't* / *don't have to* have the lights on after 10 pm.

1 You *mustn't* / *don't have to* leave the dinner table without cleaning up.

2 You *mustn't* / *don't have to* play music out loud.

3 You *mustn't* / *don't have to* wear your shoes in the bedrooms.

4 You *mustn't* / *don't have to* check out before 10 o'clock.

5 You *mustn't* / *don't have to* have breakfast at 7.30.

9 ★★☆ Match the sentences and complete them with *mustn't* or *don't have to*.

0 My parents aren't very strict.   [e]

1 Sarah hasn't got any problems with her work.   [ ]

2 The test will be hard.   [ ]

3 It's a secret.   [ ]

4 The doctor says Ella's fine.   [ ]

5 Thanks for Jim's number.   [ ]

a You _____ help her.

b I _____ forget to call him.

c You _____ tell anyone.

d She _____ take medicine any longer.

e I *don't have to* do anything in the house.

f You _____ forget to study every day now.

10 ★★★ Answer the questions so they are true for you.

1 What work do you have to do at home?

   _____

2 What are two things you mustn't do in your class?

   _____

3 Name three things you have to do during the week, but not on a Sunday.

   _____

4 What does your friend have to do that you don't have to do?

   _____

GET IT RIGHT!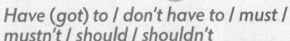

Have (got) to / don't have to / must / mustn't / should / shouldn't

We always use the base form of the verb after *have (got) to / don't have to / must / mustn't / should / shouldn't*.

✓ You **should ask** your sister to help you.

✗ You should to ask your sister to help you.

Circle the correct verb form.

1 You don't have to *making / made / make* coffee. We've got a coffee machine.

2 That music is very loud. You should *use / to use / using* headphones.

3 You must *be / to be / being* careful. It's dark in the garden.

4 He shouldn't *worry / worried / worrying* about the exam. He always gets good marks.

5 Tell Sarah she mustn't *forget / to forget / forgot* to tidy her room.

6 What do I have to *doing / do / did* to join this club?

VOCABULARY

Expressions with *like*

like (Ryan)
(it) looks like …
(it) sounds like …
Like what?

Key words in context

dream come true	Going on safari in Africa would be a **dream come true**!
illness	After a long **illness** she returned to work.
invention	The wheel was a fantastic **invention**. It changed our lives.
care about someone/something	I really **care about John.** I want to do something to help him.
environment	I think we should all protect the **environment** better.
appearance	Do you care a lot about your **appearance**?
quality	How important for you is the **quality** of your work?
inventor	Thomas Edison was a famous **inventor**.
have access to something	Do you think students should **have access to the Internet** during exams?
switch off	Let's **switch off** the computer now. It's time to relax!
robot	I'd love a **robot** that did all the housework.
create problems	You're giving him his own computer! Are you trying to **create problems**?
fair	Mum says I can't have a phone until I'm 11. It's not **fair**!

Gadgets `SB p.68`

1 ★☆☆ **Do the crossword. Can you find the mystery word?**

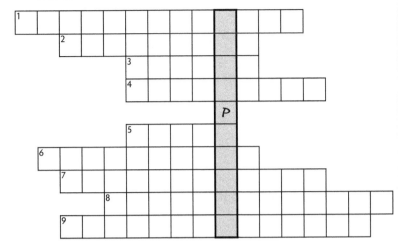

1 Many people need it to make a drink for their breakfast.
2 An electronic gadget that allows you to store music in a special format and play it.
3 Drivers use it to find their way.
4 You need it when your hair is wet.
5 A small light you hold in your hand; it usually has a battery.
6 A small electronic device that helps you with numbers.
7 The controls for a machine to play games.
8 A gadget that allows you to switch an electronic machine on or off from a distance.
9 A piece of electrical equipment to which another piece of equipment can be connected.

Housework `SB p.71`

2 ★☆☆ **Match the sentences and their endings.**

0 Luke's friends are staying for lunch. Can   **f**
1 There are no clean plates left. Can you
2 I dropped some sugar on the floor. Will you
3 My room is a mess, but I'm too lazy
4 Can you do the cooking tonight? I did it
5 I'll do the washing, but I really don't want
6 We have no food left in the house. Can you
7 Can you load the dishwasher, Sarah?
8 My mum showed me how to make my bed

a do the washing up quickly?
b yesterday, and the day before yesterday.
c to tidy it.
d when I was still a child.
e do the shopping if I tell you what we need?
f you set the table, please?
g But it's Pete's turn. I emptied it this morning.
h help me vacuum it?
i to do the ironing too.

3 ★★★ **What housework do you like/dislike? Write four sentences about you.**

I don't like ironing clothes. I think it's boring.
I don't mind doing the cooking. It's cool when the others like my food.
I hate ... . I think it's ... .

WordWise `SB p.73`

Expressions with *like*

4 ★☆☆ **Match the sentences and the pictures.**

0 Jane's like her mum. They both love nature.   **c**
1 It looks like a heart.
2 I think Dad's home. That sounds like his car!
3 It smells like an apple, but it doesn't look like one.

READING

1 REMEMBER AND CHECK (Circle) the correct option, A–C. Then check your answers in the text on page 67 of the Student's Book.

0 How did Ludwick Marishane get the idea for his invention?

   A A friend gave it to him.   **(B)** from talking with friends.   **C** He got it from the Internet.

1 What's a big problem for 2.5 billion people?

   A They've got trachoma.   **B** Their water is dirty.   **C** Medication is too expensive for them.

2 When Ludwick was at university, he spoke to a lot of people about …

   A money.   **B** his ideas.   **C** the name of his invention.

3 From the first idea to the production of 'DryBath', it took more than …

   A three years.   **B** ten years.   **C** two years.

4 Ludwick is very much interested in …

   A making money.   **B** not having to take a bath.   **C** helping people.

2 Read the article quickly. Write the name of the inventions under the photos.

Change for the better

When Emily Cummins was four years old, her grandfather gave her a hammer. She loved using it, and started to learn how to make toys from old things that nobody used any more.

When she was a teenager, she thought a lot about making inventions to help other people. Emily's other granddad had an illness called arthritis. He had a lot of pain in his hands and fingers. One day, Emily saw that he had problems getting toothpaste out of the tube. She made an invention that helped him with this, and won the Young Engineer for Britain Award for her toothpaste dispenser.

A few years later, Emily learnt about the situation in some African countries where women and children often walk many kilometres a day to get water for their villages. They can only carry one bucket a time, and they usually put them on their heads. Emily's invention is a simple water carrier. It's made of wood, so it's easy to repair. For example, the 'wheel' on the water carrier is made from branches of trees. It makes it possible for the women to transport up to five buckets each time. They don't have to carry it on their heads.

1 _____

Her latest project is a simple fridge that runs without electricity using only the energy that comes from the sun. There are now thousands of families in villages in Zambia, Namibia and South Africa who use it to keep milk, food and medicines cool.

Emily is now a young woman. She is the winner of several prizes for her inventions. She was named one of the world's top ten young people. She also got the Peace Honours Prize from a jury of Nobel prize winners during an awards ceremony in Norway.

Emily frequently visits schools and talks to teenagers. She wants to inspire them to come up with new ideas that make the world a better place. She wants to use her skills to make a difference. She isn't interested in making a bigger TV or better sound system. She wants to create change for the better.

2 _____

3 Read the article again. Are sentences 1–5 'Right' (A) or 'Wrong' (B)? If there isn't enough information to answer 'Right' or 'Wrong', choose 'Doesn't say' (C).

0	As a child, Emily loved making things herself.	**A** Right	**B** Wrong	**C** Doesn't say
1	At the age of 13, she invented a toothpaste dispenser.	**A** Right	**B** Wrong	**C** Doesn't say
2	When she went to Africa, she got an idea for a water carrier.	**A** Right	**B** Wrong	**C** Doesn't say
3	Her latest project is a solar ice cream machine.	**A** Right	**B** Wrong	**C** Doesn't say
4	Emily got a prize in Norway.	**A** Right	**B** Wrong	**C** Doesn't say
5	She'd like to invent a high quality sound system.	**A** Right	**B** Wrong	**C** Doesn't say

DEVELOPING WRITING

Taking notes and writing a short summary

1 Read the text. Tick (✓) the things that Alexander Graham Bell experimented with.

A famous inventor

When Alexander Graham Bell was 29, he made one of the most important inventions in the history of the world: the telephone. A year later, he started the Bell telephone company. It became very successful. He became a businessman and earned a lot of money from his telephone company.

But Alexander Graham Bell wasn't so interested in money. He was interested in making inventions. He always wanted to learn, and to try and create new things. He never stopped thinking of new ideas. He used his money to open laboratories with teams of engineers who could help him make his dreams come true.

Bell was also fascinated with propellers and kites, and did lots of experiments with them. In 1907, four years after the Wright Brothers made their first flight, Bell formed the Aerial Experiment Association with four young engineers. Their plan was to build planes. The group was successful. Their plane named Silver Dart made the first successful flight in Canada on 23 February, 1909.

2 Look at a student's notes on the first paragraph of the text in Exercise 1. Underline the ideas in the text that the student used.

1 29 invented telephone
2 Bell telephone company
3 success (businessman)
4 lot of money

3 Write a short text using full, connected sentences. Use the notes from Exercise 2.

4 Read the second and third paragraphs of the text about Alexander Bell again. Underline five important points and write them in the form of notes. Then write a short summary of the text based on your notes.

Writing tip: taking notes after reading a text

Read the whole text carefully.

- Go through the text again. Select the most important information. Underline it in the text and use it to write your notes.
- Write words, not sentences. Use abbreviations, e.g. *inv* for invented, *tel. co* for telephone company.
- Don't write down words that are unnecessary, e.g. *the, a, and*, etc.
- Make sure your notes are clear and meaningful. Check them again and ask yourself: Do these notes give me a good summary of the most important information in the text?
- Write up your notes.

LISTENING

1 🔊31 **Listen to the conversations. Circle A, B or C.**

1 What's the problem?

A The camera doesn't work.

B The USB cable isn't plugged in.

C The laptop doesn't work.

2 What does Daniel have to do?

A tidy his room

B walk the dog

C wash up

3 What did James borrow without asking?

A a digital camera

B an MP3 player

C a laptop

2 🔊31 **Listen again. Complete the sentences from the conversations.**

STELLA   Let ⁰m *e*_____ ¹s_____. You
²h_____ ³t_____ switch
⁴y_____ ⁵c_____ on.

DANIEL   Alright. ⁶G_____ you. Do I
⁷h_____ to ⁸t_____ up my
desk ⁹t_____?

LILY   Well, you ¹⁰m_____ use
¹¹m_____ ¹²th_____ without
¹³a_____.

DIALOGUE

1 **Complete the conversation with the expressions in the list.**

do you mean | Like what | Sorry

OLIVER   I want to do a mini-triathlon on Sunday.

MAYA   ¹_____?

OLIVER   A mini-triathlon. That's three races in one.

MAYA   Three races in one? What
²_____?

OLIVER   Well, you have to run 3 km, swim 1 km, and cycle 10 km.

MAYA   Really? That sounds like hard work. Why is it called mini?

OLIVER   Because the races in a normal triathlon are much longer.

MAYA   ³_____?

OLIVER   Well, in the Olympic triathlon they cycle 40 km, run 10 km, and swim 1.5 km.

MAYA   Wow! I think we should try the mini race!

OLIVER   I think you're right.

2 **Write a short conversation for this picture. Use some of the expressions from Listening Exercise 2 and Dialogue Exercise 1.**

PHRASES FOR FLUENCY SB p.73

1 **Complete the conversation with the expressions in the list.**

so | no chance | and stuff | never mind

absolutely | such good fun

MAX   ⁰____*So*____, Isaac, what are you doing after school?

ISAAC   After school? Why?

MAX   I just want to know if you want to play football.

ISAAC   Football! ¹_____, I've got to do housework ²_____.

MAX   OK, ³_____. What about tomorrow? Can we play then?

ISAAC   ⁴_____.

MAX   Great. It's going to be ⁵_____!

Pronunciation

Vowel sounds: /ʊ/ and /uː/

Go to page 120.

Reading and Writing part 1

1 Match the notices A–H with the meanings 1–5.

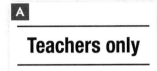
A Teachers only

B Under 12s half price

C Please DON'T feed the monkeys.

D Wanted – waiter
••• Please enquire inside.

E DANGER look out for trains

F SALE 50% off everything

G SWIMMING POOL closed from 19th Oct – 12th Nov

H Keep off the grass

0	Be careful when you cross here.	E
1	Children pay less than adults.	
2	You mustn't give food to the animals.	
3	If you are interested in the job, come in and ask for more details.	
4	School children can't come in here.	
5	Things in this shop are half price.	

2 Match the notices A–H with the meanings 1–5.

A Chocolate £2 each or 3 for £5

B Baby rabbits – free to good homes

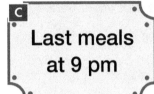
C Last meals at 9 pm

D All food is homemade

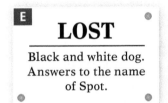
E LOST Black and white dog. Answers to the name of Spot.

F PLEASE DON'T PHONE BEFORE 12 PM

G Magic Car Race get yours here on Saturday morning.

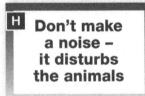
H Don't make a noise – it disturbs the animals

0	We're looking for our pet.	E
1	You should only call them in the afternoons.	
2	You can buy the new game this weekend.	
3	It's cheaper to buy more than one.	
4	Please be quiet here.	
5	If you want to eat here, order before nine.	

Exam guide: match notices with meanings

In this exam task you have to read some notices and then match them to sentences that describe what each notice says.

- Read through all the notices. Tick the ones that you think you understand best. Look at these ones first. Try to think how you would describe what they say. Then look through the answers to see if any of them match what you think.

- If you're not 100% sure what a notice means then focus on some of the words in it that you do understand. Try to match or connect these with words in the sentences. For example, teachers and school children are obviously connected so there's a good chance these two belong together.

- Be careful – there are always more notices than sentences.

GRAMMAR

Past continuous SB p.76

1 ★☆☆ **Complete the text with *was* or *were*.**

It was a cold winter's morning. It ⁰____*was*____ raining a little. Mums and dads ¹_____ standing by the school football field. They ²_____ chatting and drinking coffee to keep warm. They ³_____ waiting for the game to begin. On the field, their daughters ⁴_____ getting ready for the big match. Some of them ⁵_____ running and others ⁶_____ kicking balls about. The goalkeeper ⁷_____ practising catching the ball. Everyone was excited. It was the final of the under 16s girls football tournament. Mr Fletcher, the headmaster, ⁸_____ cleaning his glasses. He put them on, took the whistle out of his pocket, and blew it.

2 ★★☆ **Complete the text. Choose the correct words and write them in the correct form.**

jump | take | cry | clap | sit | hold
not feel | talk | not enjoy

I got there very late. The game was over. The girls of Blacon High School ⁰*were jumping* up and down. They were the champions. Their proud parents ¹_____. One girl ²_____ up the trophy and showing it to the crowd. She wasn't being very careful and I was afraid she might drop the trophy, but luckily she didn't. A journalist ³_____ lots of photos. But not everyone was happy. The girls on the losing team ⁴_____ on the ground. Some of them had their heads in their hands and they ⁵_____. They certainly ⁶_____ the celebrations. Mr Fletcher ⁷_____ to them but they ⁸_____ great. Another year and still no trophy.

Pronunciation

Strong and weak forms of *was* and *were*
Go to page 120. ◀))

3 ★★★ **Complete the sentences. Use the past continuous of the verbs and the information in brackets.**

0   Paula *wasn't watching TV*, she *was playing games* .
    (– watch TV / + playing games)

1   I_____, I_____.
    (– write an email / + write my blog)

2   They_____, they
    _____.
    (– speak Polish / + speak Russian)

3   We_____, we_____.
    (– fight / + play)

4   Dad_____, he_____.
    (– read / + listen to the radio)

4 ★☆☆ **Match the questions and answers.**

0   Were you listening to me?   [d]
1   Was he laughing?   [ ]
2   Was it raining?   [ ]
3   Were they talking?   [ ]
4   Was I sleeping?   [ ]
5   Were we making a lot of noise?   [ ]

a   Yes, it was. We got really wet.
b   Yes they were but I didn't hear what they said.
c   Yes, I think you were.
d   Yes, I heard everything you said.
e   No, I don't think we were.
f   No, he wasn't. He didn't think it was very funny.

5 ★★☆ **Answer the questions so they are true for you.**

What were you doing …

1   at 7 am today?
    _____

2   at 6 pm yesterday?
    _____

3   this time yesterday?
    _____

4   at 10 o'clock last Sunday morning?
    _____

Past continuous vs. past simple `SB p.79`

6 ★☆☆ **Match the sentence halves.**

0 While the teacher was talking, `e`

1 Evan was drinking coffee ☐

2 The boys were fighting ☐

3 They were looking at the map ☐

4 While I was reading in the bath, ☐

5 I was brushing my teeth ☐

a and he burned his mouth.

b when their mum walked into the room.

c I dropped my book in the water.

d but my toothbrush broke.

e I put my hand up to ask a question.

f when they realised they were lost.

7 ★★☆ **Circle the correct words.**

0 Matthew *played* / (*was playing*) the guitar when he (*fell*) / *was falling* off the stage.

1 I *did* / *was doing* my homework when my sister *came* / *was coming* into the room.

2 John and his sister *walked* / *were walking* to school when the accident *happened* / *was happening*.

3 I *talked* / *was talking* about Kiki when she *phoned* / *was phoning* me.

4 While Anna *tidied* / *was tidying* up her room, she *found* / *was finding* her watch.

5 While Alison *studied* / *was studying*, she *remembered* / *was remembering* it was her mum's birthday.

6 When we *found* / *were finding* out about the accident, *we watched* / *were watching* TV.

when and *while* `SB p.79`

8 ★★☆ **Complete the sentences with *when* or *while*.**

0 ___*While*___ I was trying to get to sleep, the dog started barking.

1 She was eating an apple _____ she bit her tongue.

2 We were driving in the car _____ we saw Robin on his bike.

3 _____ I was paying for the T-shirt, I realised I didn't have any money.

4 Olivia was having dinner _____ the phone rang.

5 _____ I was walking into town, I saw I had different socks on.

9 ★★★ **Write two sentences about each picture.**

0 Paul / jog / trip over / stone
While Paul was jogging, he tripped over a stone.
Paul was jogging when he tripped over a stone.

1 Gordon / rock-climb / drop / bag

_____

_____

2 May / windsurfing / fall / sea

_____

_____

3 Sue / volleyball / run into / net

_____

_____

GET IT RIGHT! ◉

Past continuous

We form the past continuous with *was/were* + the *-ing* form of the verb. We use *was* with singular subjects and *were* with plural subjects.

✓ We **were playing** football when it started to rain.

✗ We ~~was~~ playing football when it started to rain.

✓ I **was windsurfing** when the accident happened.

✗ I ~~were~~ windsurfing when the accident happened.

Complete the sentences with *was* or *were*.

1 The rain started while they _____ having a picnic.

2 My friends and I _____ enjoying the competition, when the TV stopped working.

3 My brother _____ winning the race when he fell off his bike.

4 _____ you driving when it started to snow?

VOCABULARY

Sports

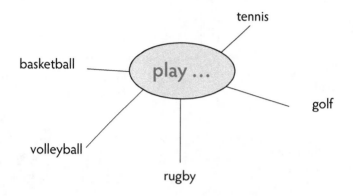

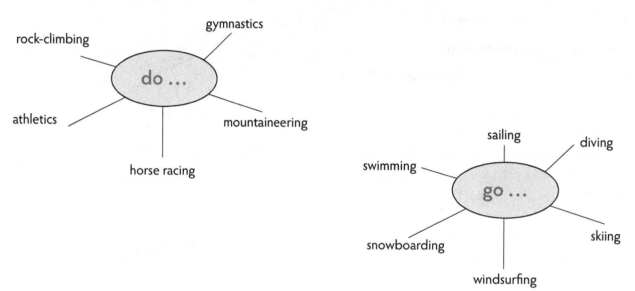

Sequencing

at first ➜ then ➜ after ➜ finally

Key words in context

marathon	The **marathon** is just over 42 km.
spectator	More than 100,000 **spectators** watched the final.
athlete	There are **athletes** from all over the world at the Olympics.
medal (bronze, silver, gold)	We didn't win a **medal** but we had a lot of fun.
stadium	The **stadium** was completely full. There wasn't an empty seat anywhere.
trophy	The captain put the **trophy** above his head and showed it to the spectators.
goal	I scored the winning **goal** in the last minute of the match.
winner	The **winner** of each race gets a gold medal.
accident	The driver had a serious **accident** but luckily no-one was hurt.
shine	The sun **is shining**. Let's go to the beach.
dream	My **dream** is to play football for Manchester United one day.
practise	You need to **practise** every day if you want to be the best.
competitive	My dad's so **competitive**. He always wants to win.
lose control	The driver **lost control** of the car and crashed into a wall.
take place	The 2014 World Cup **took place** in Brazil.
cross	The first person to **cross** the line is the winner.
grab	She **grabbed** the dog to stop it from running away.

Sports `SB p.76`

1 ★★☆ Use the picture clues to find the sports, then fit the sports into the word lines. The black boxes contain the last letter of one word and the first letter of the next word. There are four sports that don't fit in the word lines. What are they?

1 _____ 2 _____ 3 _____ 4 _____

| | | | | | | | S | | | | | | | | | | |

| | | | | G | | | | | | S | | | | | | | |

| | | | S | | | | G | | F | | | | | | | |

2 ★★★ Which sport is the odd one out in each list, and why?

0 tennis / rugby / windsurfing / basketball
   Answer: _*windsurfing*_ , because
   the other sports all use balls.

1 skiing / snowboarding / swimming / ski jumping
   Answer: _____, because
   _____.

2 windsurfing / rock-climbing / sailing / diving
   Answer: _____, because
   _____.

3 tennis / rugby / volleyball / football
   Answer: _____, because
   _____.

3 ★★☆ Write sentences. Use the expressions in the list to start each sentence.

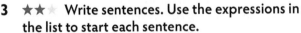
~~At first~~ | Finally | Then | After half an hour

0 nervous
   At first, I was nervous.

1 instructor / show / what to do
   _____

2 could stand up
   _____

3 ski / down the hill
   _____

4 ★★★ Write a mini-story. Use the expressions and your own ideas.

The Tennis Game

1 At first ...   3 After ...
2 Then ...   4 Finally ...

READING

1 **REMEMBER AND CHECK** Answer the questions.
Then check your answers in the article on page 75
of the Student's Book.

0 How long was the race Derek Redmond was
running in? *400 metres*

1 How far did he run before his accident? _____

2 How many people were there in the athletics stadium?

_____

3 How high is the mountain K2? _____

4 How far from the top did Gerlinde Kaltenbrunner
get in the summer of 2010? _____

5 How many times did she climb K2 before she was successful?

_____

2 Read the article. Match the high jumping styles with the names in *italics*.

People who changed sport: Dick Fosbury

Like many American teenagers, Dick Fosbury wanted to be a professional sportsman but he had a problem – he wasn't very good at any sport. He didn't play football very well and although he was very tall he wasn't a very good basketball player either. He decided to try athletics. He tried running, throwing and jumping, and of all these events, he found that he wasn't too bad at the high jump.

At that time there were two popular styles of jumping over the bar. There was *the scissors*, where the athlete jumped over using his legs like a pair of scissors, and there was *the straddle*, where the athlete jumped over face first. Fosbury used the straddle. The best height he could jump was 1.63 m. It wasn't bad but it was a long way from the world record of 2.23 m.

One afternoon Fosbury decided to do something completely different.

Instead of jumping face first, he turned around and jumped back first. The results were amazing. In a few hours he improved his personal best by 21 cm. Over the next months he spent all his time practising, getting better and better. He still wasn't winning any competitions and most people were confused by his strange style. A year before the 1968 Olympics he was the number 61 jumper in the

world, and he only just made it into the USA Olympic team.

When he arrived in Mexico no one knew his name. On the day of the high jump final he walked on to the field with all the other jumpers. As the competition started, the 80,000 people in the crowd began to notice that one of the jumpers had a very strange style. At first they thought it was funny and laughed each time Fosbury jumped over the bar. After nearly four hours there were only three jumpers left. The crowd weren't laughing at Fosbury any more – they were cheering him on. The bar was at 2.24 m – a new world record. The other two jumpers knocked it off but Fosbury flew over. The gold medal was his.

Dick Fosbury was now famous all over the world and his *Fosbury flop* changed forever the way that high jumpers jumped.

3 Read the article again. Answer the questions.

0 Why did Fosbury choose to do the high jump?
Because it was the only sport that
he wasn't bad at.

1 How high could he jump after a few hours
practising his new style?

_____

2 What did people first think about his new style?

3 How good was he at the high jump in 1967?

_____

4 Was he the favourite to win the gold medal in the
Olympics? Explain your answer.

_____

5 How do people remember Dick Fosbury today?

_____

DEVELOPING WRITING

An article

1 **Read the text below. Where do you think it comes from?**

a   A newspaper ☐

b   A school magazine ☐

c   A holiday magazine ☐

d   A story book ☐

2 **Read the text again. Where do these missing phrases go?**

0   and when we arrived, we weren't disappointed   A

1   I was soon climbing up and down the rocks. ☐

2   and we had to stop ☐

3   No-one really wanted to get onto the coach. ☐

4   and of the spectacular ocean on the other ☐

3 **Write an article for a school magazine (about 120–150 words). Choose one of these topics.**

● A sports match between your school and another one

● A school trip

● A special event that happened at the school

Fun and adventure in North Wales

Last week, year 12 students spent four nights at the Mini-Don adventure centre in North Wales. There was a lot of excitement on the coach journey there A . The centre is in a small wood. It has views of the magnificent Welsh mountains on one side B . We put our bags in the bedrooms, had some lunch, and then we met our friendly instructors.

Over the four days we had the chance to try out some really exciting new sports. In the mornings I chose rock-climbing. At first I was quite scared, but my instructor, Dave, was really good at keeping me calm. C In the afternoons I did windsurfing. It was quite difficult. On the last day I was starting to get quite good when unfortunately the weather got bad D . Now I really want to take lessons here so I can get really good at it.

It was a shame to say goodbye to the centre on Friday morning. E We had a wonderful time and if you ever get the chance to go there – take it!

LISTENING

1 🔊36 Listen to the street interviews. Who does, or wants to do, these sports, the girl (G) or the boy (B)?

0 G

1

2

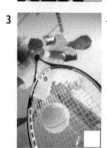
3

4

5

6

7

8

2 🔊36 Listen again. Mark the sentences T (true) or F (false).

0 The girl thinks the sports centre looks good. ☐ T

1 The girl isn't very interested in sport. ☐

2 You can do water sports at the sports centre. ☐

3 The boy thinks the building cost too much. ☐

4 The sports centre has a golf course. ☐

DIALOGUE

1 Put the words in order to make questions and answers.

0 about / sports / do / think / What / centre / you / the / new
What do you think about the new sports centre?

1 brilliant / think / I / it's

2 sports / do / feel / you / centre / How / the / about / new

3 money / of / I / a / waste / it's / think

---

2 Put the sentences in order to complete the conversation.

DAN Well, we need a new swimming pool. ☐

DAN I don't agree. ☐

DAN What do you think about the new library? ☐ 1

DAN I think it's a waste of money. There are better things to spend our money on. ☐

ANA For example? ☐

ANA I like it. I think it's really good for our town. ☐

ANA So what do you feel about it then? ☐

ANA I'm sorry but I think a library is more important than a swimming pool. ☐

▰▰▰ TRAIN TO THiNK ▰▰▰

Sequencing

1 Look at the words 1–4 in table A and the groups A–E in table B.

a What group does each word belong to?

b What position [1], [2], [3] or [4] does each word take in the group?

Table A

	Group	Position
0 afternoon	C	2
1 baby		
2 today		
3 Saturday		
4 wake up		

Table B

Group A	[1] child	[2] teenager	[3] adult	[4]
Group B	[1] Monday	[2] Wednesday	[3] Friday	[4]
Group C	[1] morning	[2] evening	[3] night	[4]
Group D	[1] go to school	[2] have lunch	[3] come home	[4]
Group E	[1] yesterday	[2] tomorrow	[3] next weekend	[4]

2 Put the lists of words in order. Add one more item at the end of each list.

0 October / March / June
March, June, October, (November)

1 third / second / fourth

2 ask for the bill / look at the menu / order your meal

3 sometimes / often / rarely

Listening parts 4 and 5

1 ◀))37 You will hear a woman, Sally, asking about a women's football team. Listen and complete each question.

AFC Women's Football Club

Name:	AFC Women's Football Club
Training day:	0 *Thursday*
Time:	1 _____
Cost:	2£_____
Contact:	John 3_____
Phone number:	4 _____

2 ◀))38 You will hear a man talking about the London Olympic stadium. Listen and complete each question.

The London 2012 Olympic stadium

Distance from London – 0 _____ **10** _____ km

Work started – 1 22 _____ , 2008

Work finished – 2 _____

First event – celebrity 3 _____

Cost – 4£_____ million

Capacity – third 5 _____ stadium in the UK

Exam guide: listening – filling in notes

In the KEY listening parts 4 and 5 you must listen to a text and then complete some notes about it. The only difference between the two parts is that part 4 is a conversation between two people while part 5 is a monologue (just one person talking).

- Before you listen look at the form you have to fill in. Look at the title and the questions. This tells you what the listening is about and helps you prepare.
- Look closely at the spaces you have to fill in on the form. You have to fill in each one with a word or a figure (for example, a date, a price or a number). What kind of information do you think is missing?
- You will hear the missing information in the order that it appears on the form. If you miss something, don't worry. You will have a second chance to hear it again.
- Use the first listening to write in as many of the answers as you can. Use the second listening to check these answers and focus on any that are missing.

CONSOLIDATION

LISTENING

1 🔊39 **Listen to the conversation. Circle A, B or C.**

1 What kind of lesson is Lucy going to the sports centre for?
 A gym
 B rock climbing
 C swimming

2 What is in the bathroom?
 A a hairdryer
 B an MP3 player
 C headphones

3 What is on the living room floor?
 A magazines
 B a games console
 C a docking station

2 🔊39 **Listen again. Answer the questions.**

0 How long is it until Lucy's lesson starts?
 Two hours.

1 Why does she want to go to the sports centre earlier?

2 What does her dad want her to do?

3 What was Lucy's dad doing when he sat on the headphones?

4 Where is Lucy's MP3 player?

5 Where does he want Lucy to help him?

6 Why does he think cutting wood is a good idea for Lucy?

VOCABULARY

3 **Unscramble the letters. Write the words.**

0 I'd love to go *nagilis*, but I can't swim and I'm scared I might fall in the water. _*sailing*_

1 We don't all want to listen to your music. Put your *oehadpenhs* on. _____

2 I can't do this sum. Have you got a *alaclutocr*?
 _____

3 I tried to play *fogl* once, but I couldn't even hit the ball. _____

4 I can't see anything. Have you got a *corth*?
 _____

GRAMMAR

4 **Complete the sentences. Use the correct form of the verbs in brackets.**

0 They _____*had*_____ (have) the accident while they *were programming* (program) the satnav.

1 I _____ (tidy) up my bedroom when I _____ (find) my torch.

2 She _____ (use) the coffee machine when she _____ (burn) her hand.

3 Dad _____ (tell) us to do our homework when we _____ (play) on the game console.

4 I _____ (listen) to my MP3 player when it _____ (stop) working.

5 **Circle the correct words.**

DAD Hey, Ben, why are you looking so sad?

BEN We lost the match.

DAD You ⁰*shouldn't* / must worry so much. You ¹*mustn't always* / *don't always* have to win.

BEN Yes, but we never win. We ²*should* / *don't have to* try to win sometimes. Our coach says we ³*shouldn't* / *must* try harder. He thinks we ⁴*should* / *mustn't* have extra training sessions.

DAD What! You already have three. Is he crazy? I think I ⁵*shouldn't* / *have to* have a chat with him.

BEN It's OK, Dad. You ⁶*mustn't* / *don't have to* do that. I don't think I want to play for the team anymore.

DAD Come on, Ben, you ⁷*shouldn't* / *must* give up so easily.

BEN But you always told me that you ⁸*should* / *don't have to* love what you do. I don't even like playing football.

DAD Well, you ⁹*must* / *shouldn't* always listen to what I say. Sometimes even I get it wrong.

DIALOGUE

6 **Complete the conversation. Use the words in the list.**

~~should~~ | windsurfing | sorry | tell | mean
skiing | fear | doing | what | do

ANNA I'm bored.

DAN You ⁰___*should*___ get yourself a hobby, then.

ANNA Like ¹_____?

DAN Well, maybe you could start doing a sport.

ANNA You ²_____, do some exercise?

DAN Exactly. What about a water sport? Sailing or ³_____, or something like that.

ANNA But I've got aquaphobia – you know, a fear of water.

DAN OK, what about rock-climbing? They ⁴_____ lessons at the gym.

ANNA No, I've got acrophobia.

DAN ⁵_____?

ANNA Acrophobia – it's a ⁶_____ of heights.

DAN Snowboarding? ⁷_____?

ANNA No, I've got chionophobia.

DAN Don't ⁸_____ me – a fear of snow.

ANNA Exactly.

DAN I think you've got lazyitus.

ANNA What's that?

DAN The fear of ⁹_____ any exercise!

READING

7 **Read the text. Match the titles with the paragraphs.**

0 The prizes [C]   2 Try saying this! [ ]

1 The places [ ]   3 Young and old [ ]

All you need to know about the Olympic Games in 150 words

A London is the only city to hold the Games three times (1908, 1948 and 2012). The USA held them four times but in three different cities.

B At the Paris Games in 1900, there were more athletes than spectators. The oldest athlete ever at the games was Sweden's Oscar Swahn. He won a silver medal in shooting in 1920 at the age of 72. The youngest medal winner was Inge Sorensen from Denmark. She was 12 when she won a bronze medal in swimming.

C In the first modern Olympic Games, in Athens in 1896, there were no gold medals. The winners all got silver medals. In the 1900 Games, the winners got trophies instead of medals. Winners first got gold medals in the 1904 Olympics in St Louis, USA.

D And finally, the longest name for an Olympic champion was Prapawadee Jaroenrattanatarakoon from Thailand. She won a gold medal in weightlifting.

WRITING

8 **Choose a sport or a sportsperson that you like. Write a text called 'All you need to know about …' (about 150 words).**

- Choose some interesting trivia.
- Try to organise it into three or four short paragraphs.
- Can you do it in 150 words exactly?

GRAMMAR

Comparative adjectives `SB p.86`

1 ★☆☆ **Write the comparative form of the adjectives.**

0 old ___*older*___   5 good _____

1 bad _____   6 happy _____

2 beautiful _____   7 interesting _____

3 easy _____   8 nice _____

4 expensive _____   9 young _____

2 ★★☆ **Complete the B sentences. Use the comparative form of the adjectives in the A sentences.**

0 A Question number 1 is difficult.

   B Yes, it is – but question number 2 is ___*more difficult*___ !

1 A Was your laptop expensive?

   B Yes, it was, but the old one was _____ .

2 A She's young.

   B Yes, but her sister's _____ than her.

3 A This book's interesting.

   B You're right, but the other one is _____ .

4 A Wow – that's a good camera.

   B It's not bad. Actually, I want to buy a _____ one than this!

5 A This film's bad!

   B Yes, but the other one was _____ !

3 ★★☆ **Complete the sentences. Use the comparative form of the adjectives in brackets.**

	Sandra	Justine
Age:	12	13
Height:	1.58	1.56
Does homework:	sometimes	always
English score:	93%	74%

0 Sandra is *younger than* Justine. (young)

1 Sandra is _____ Justine. (tall)

2 Justine is _____ Sandra. (hard-working)

3 Sandra is _____ at English _____ Justine. (good)

4 ★★★ **Write comparative sentences using your own ideas. Use the words in brackets to help you.**

1 your school / another school in your town (*big / good …?*)

   _____

2 you / your best friend (*old / tall / intelligent …?*)

   _____

3 two TV programmes (*funny / long / exciting …?*)

   _____

4 (any two things you want to compare)

   _____

can / can't for ability `SB p.87`

5 ★☆☆ **Look at the pictures. Write a sentence for each picture.**

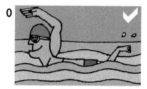

0 He *can swim*.   1 He _____

2 She _____   3 He _____

6 ★★☆ **Write sentences so they are true for you. Use the verbs in the list to help you, or other verbs you know.**

~~sing~~ | ~~speak French~~ | walk | run fast
play the guitar | fly | swim

0 I can ___*sing*___ , but I can't ___*speak French*___ .

1 I can't _____ , but I can _____ .

2 My father can _____ , but he can't _____ .

3 My best friend can _____ , but he/she can't _____ .

4 Birds can _____ , but they can't _____ .

Superlative adjectives SB p.88

7 ★☆☆ **Complete the conversations. Use the phrases in the list.**

~~the laziest~~ | the best | the oldest | the worst
the most expensive | the most interesting
the most difficult

0 **A** Who's _the laziest_ kid in your class?
  B Steve. He never does anything!

1 **A** That test was hard!
  B It was. In fact it was _____ test this year.

2 **A** Do you think they're a good band?
  B Yes, I do. They're _____ band around at the moment.

3 **A** That's a great shirt.
  B Yes, it's really nice. But I can't buy it. It's _____ shirt in the shop!

4 **A** What a horrible day. Rain, rain, rain.
  B Yes, I think it's _____ day of the summer.

5 **A** Who's _____ person in your family?
  B Grandpa. He's 74.

6 **A** You really like History, don't you?
  B Yes, I think it's _____ subject at school.

8 ★★☆ Circle **the correct words.**

0 Is the Amazon *longer* / *the longest* river in the world?

1 Alex is *taller* / *the tallest* than me.

2 Yesterday was *colder* / *the coldest* day of the year.

3 My father is *younger* / *the youngest* than my mother.

4 He wants to be *richer* / *the richest* person in the country.

5 Is this exercise *more difficult* / *the most difficult* on this page?

9 ★★☆ **Complete the sentences. Use the superlative form of the adjectives in the list.**

~~rich~~ | boring | delicious | high
fast | important | strong

0 She's got a really big house and a Porsche. She's _the richest_ person I know!

1 He can pick up a 50 kilo bag of potatoes. He's _____ man I know.

2 I almost fell asleep in the film. It was _____ film out for a long time!

3 Wow! This fish is so good! It's _____ food that my mother makes!

4 This car does 280 kph. Maybe it's _____ car in the world.

5 Which is _____ mountain in the world?

6 Some people say that the day you get married is _____ day of your life.

10 ★★★ **Write one comparative sentence and one superlative sentence about the things in each group, using your own ideas. Use the adjectives in the list to help you.**

~~cold~~ | ~~hot~~ | healthy | enjoyable | delicious
fast | cheap | interesting | good | difficult
boring | big

0 winter – summer – autumn
  Summer is hotter than autumn.
  Winter's the coldest time of the year.

1 running – football – swimming
  _____
  _____

2 pizza – chips – salad
  _____
  _____

3 music – films – books
  _____
  _____

4 Brazil – China – Britain
  _____
  _____

5 train – plane – bus
  _____
  _____

GET IT RIGHT!
Comparative and superlative adjectives

We form the comparative of <u>long</u> adjectives with *more* + adjective. We form the comparative of <u>short</u> adjectives (one syllable) with adjective + *-er*. Don't use *more* with adjective + *-er*.

✓ My cousin is **younger** than me.

✗ My cousin is ~~more younger~~ than me.

We form the superlative of <u>long</u> adjectives with (*the*) *most* + adjective. We form the superlative of <u>short</u> adjectives (one syllable) with *the* + adjective + *-est*. Don't use (*the*) *most* with short adjective + *-est*.

✓ It was **the coldest** winter in history.

✗ It was the ~~most coldest winter~~ in history.

Complete the text with the comparative or superlative form of the adjectives in brackets.

I love climbing mountains. For me, it's [1] _____ (exciting) hobby. I think [2] _____ (beautiful) mountains in the world are in New Zealand. But [3] _____ (tall) mountains in the world are in Asia. The mountains in England are [4] _____ (small) than in Asia and the weather is [5] _____ (cold). The USA has [6] _____ (warm) weather than England, but Asia's weather is [7] _____ (hot). So, I love going climbing in Asia.

VOCABULARY

The weather

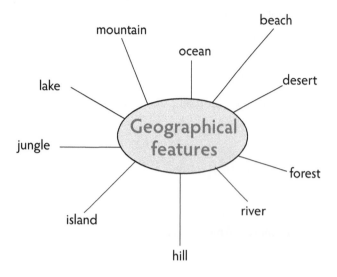

mountain
beach
ocean
lake
desert
jungle
Geographical features
forest
river
island
hill

cloudy

cold

humid

foggy

freezing

hot

Phrases with *with*

to be **busy with** something

(to have nothing) **to do with** (me)

to **be with** someone

to **be good with** something (e.g. animals / children)

a place **with** (big rooms / lots of animals / lots of tourists)

dry

rainy

Key words in context

attractive	The butterfly is a beautiful blue and red insect – it's very **attractive**.
brave	When the lion attacked the girl, a **brave** man helped her.
courage	I wanted to talk to the President, but I didn't have the **courage**.
dangerous	It's a **dangerous** animal – don't go near it, it might bite you.
extreme	There was a 150 kph wind! That's really **extreme** weather.
ice	Be careful! It was very cold last night and there's **ice** on the roads.
medicine	He was ill so we went to the chemist's to buy some **medicine** for him.
on record	Last night was the coldest night **on record** in this country.
temperature	Sometimes the **temperature** goes up to 37° Celsius.

sunny

warm

wet

windy

Geographical features SB p.86

1 ★★☆ **Match the words and the definitions.**

ᵃforest | ᵇisland | ᶜhill | ᵈdesert | ᵉbeach | ᶠjungle
ᵍocean | ʰriver | ⁱlake | ʲmountain

0	a place with lots of trees growing together	a
1	an area of sand (or rocks) near the sea	
2	a bit of land with water all round it	
3	a high bit of land (not as high as a mountain)	
4	water that moves across the land and into the sea	
5	a very high piece of land	
6	a big area of water with land around it	
7	a very large area of sea water	
8	an area in a hot country with trees and plants close together and wild animals	
9	a big, hot, dry area of land (often with sand)	

2 ★★★ **Use the words in Exercise 1 to complete the sentences. Make the words plural if you need to.**

0 It's important to take lots of water with you if you go into the _____ desert _____.

1 Madagascar is a very big _____ in the Indian Ocean.

2 I love sitting on a _____ and swimming in the sea.

3 The longest _____ in the world is the Nile.

4 The Himalayas has the highest _____ in the world.

5 I was very tired after I cycled up the _____.

6 Let's go for a walk in the _____ and look for wild mushrooms!

7 We took a small boat and went round the _____.

8 Tigers live in the _____ in India and Indonesia.

9 The ship hit a rock and went to the bottom of the _____.

The weather SB p.89

3 ★☆☆ **Complete the 'weather' words with the missing letters.**

1 Yesterday was c _o_ _l_ _d_ but today it's really f _ _ _ zin _! It's a bit w _ _ _ y too.

2 It was nice and w _ _ _ yesterday. But today is even
better: it's s _ _ ny, h _ t and d _ y!

3 It's a horrible day today. It's c _ _ _ dy and cold. This morning it was r _ _ _ y so it's w _ t here, too.

4 When it's f _ _ _ _ like today, it's hard to see where you're going!

4 ★★☆ **Use the words in Exercise 3 to complete the text.**

I'm from Britain but I live in Brasilia, the capital of Brazil. The weather here is usually good – the temperature is normally between about 12 degrees and 28 degrees Celcius, so it's never really
⁰ _____ cold _____. Some days in summer it's really
¹h_____, but a lot of the time it's just nice and ²w_____, especially in the evenings.

There is one period in the year – from about May to July or August – when it just doesn't rain! So everything is very ³d_____. At other times of the year, the weather can be ⁴r_____ – and when it rains, it rains really hard!

Some days in the morning, when you wake up, the sky is grey and ⁵c_____, but then the clouds go away and the morning can be bright and ⁶s_____.

So, the weather here is quite nice really – not like my home country, Britain, where it's ⁷f_____ some days in winter!

WordWise SB p.91

Phrases with *with*

5 ★☆☆ **Complete the sentences. Use the phrases in the list.**

with 220 bedrooms | busy with
with tomato sauce | good with
to do with you | with you

0 It's a big hotel _with 220 bedrooms_.

1 A Isn't Alice here?
  B No. I thought she came _____.

2 It's delicious – pasta _____ and chicken.

3 She looks after my little brother. She's really _____ children.

4 Please don't ask me about it. It's got nothing _____.

5 I phoned him but he didn't answer. He was _____ his homework.

READING

1 REMEMBER AND CHECK Match the phrases to make sentences. Then check your answers in the article on page 85 of the Student's Book.

0	The San people	in small houses	and tell stories about hunting.
1	When they are ill,	near a fire	from the older people.
2	The people in the tribe live	difficult for people and animals	from plants.
3	San children have to learn	San bushmen	with bows and arrows.
4	In the evening, the San people sit	hunt animals	to show them the places and animals.
5	In the Kalahari, life can be	they get medicine	because it's very dry.
6	Tourists to the Kalahari often have	about the dangers around them	made from wood and grass.

2 Read the information. Mark the sentences T (true) or F (false).

0 The Inuit do not move around like they did in the past. ☐ T

1 The Inuit get their food from hunting and fishing. ☐

2 Inuit houses made of ice are called igloos. ☐

3 A harpoon is a kind of animal. ☐

4 The Inuit still use sledges, but not with dogs. ☐

The Inuit – in the past and nowadays

The Inuit are people who live in the north of Canada, the USA and Greenland, in a place of snow and ice.

	In the past	Nowadays
Living Areas	In the past, the Inuit people lived in camps and they moved all the time, depending on the weather.	Now they live in fixed communities, groups of houses mostly near the sea and at the mouths of rivers.
Homes	The Inuit people lived in tents made from animal skins, or in igloos (traditional houses made of ice).	These days they live in wooden houses that are built in the south of Canada. But they still use tents, too, next to the houses, and igloos when they are hunting.
Clothes	They wore clothes made from the skin or fur of the animals that they killed.	Now the Inuit mostly wear modern, ready-made clothes, but they still also use traditional fur boots, gloves and clothes, especially in the winter.
Food Supply	The Inuit got their food by hunting and fishing, using bows and arrows but also harpoons (special tools for killing fish or seals). They also caught animals that they could eat, using traps.	Now, the Inuit continue to hunt and fish but they usually get their food using guns and modern fishing equipment.
Transport	They had dogs that carried things and that also pulled the sledges for people to move around. On the rivers, they used kayaks (a special boat for one or two people).	Now they use sledges with motors and their boats also have motors. And in the communities, they use cars.

3 Read the text again. Are the facts 1–5 true about only the past, only the present, or both? Tick (✓) the boxes.

		Only the past	Only the present	Both past and present
0	Living in camps	✓	☐	☐
1	Living in igloos	☐	☐	☐
2	Wearing clothes made of fur	☐	☐	☐
3	Using guns	☐	☐	☐
4	Using dogs	☐	☐	☐
5	Using boats	☐	☐	☐

DEVELOPING WRITING

An informal email

1 Read Jake's email to Monika. Answer the questions.

1 Where is Monika going on holiday?

2 Which two places does Jake recommend?

Hey Monika,

Great to get your email yesterday. So, your summer holiday will be in Thailand? That's wonderful! I hope you have a fantastic time.

Maybe you know (or maybe not?) that I went to Thailand two years ago with my family. It's a great place and I enjoyed it a lot. Food, people, places – so different from Europe!

Anyway, I'm writing to give you some ideas. People usually arrive in Bangkok and stay there a few days. Well, when you are in Bangkok, don't miss the Royal Palace! It's just fabulous, I'm attaching a photo I took. You have to go there!

And if you like beaches and swimming and things – and I think you do! – then make sure you go to the Phi Phi Islands. They're in the south of Thailand and you can swim and go diving and see lots of wonderful fish. It's very beautiful there and it's a great place to relax. I'd really recommend it!

Well, I have to go now, but if you want any more ideas, please write to me, OK?

Your friend,

Jake

PS You mustn't forget to take your camera to Thailand, OK!?

---

2 Read Jake's email again. <u>Underline</u> the adjectives that he uses to give his opinion of things in Thailand.

1 Are the adjectives positive or negative?

2 Does Jake use any adjectives that are new for you? Look them up in a dictionary if you need to.

3 Complete the phrases that Jake uses. What is he doing when he writes these things?

0 ___*Don't*___ miss the Royal Palace.

1 You _____ go there!

2 _____ you go to the Phi Phi Islands.

3 I'd really _____ it.

4 You _____ forget to take your camera!

Pronunciation

Vowel sounds: /ɪ/ and /aɪ/

Go to page 120. 🔊

4 You are going to write an email to an English-speaking friend and tell them about a place that you know and that you really like. (You can imagine that you know the place.) Plan your email. Think about the place you want to write about.

- What is special about it?
- What adjectives do you want to use to describe it?
- What things or places there do you want to recommend to your friend?
- What do you think your friend should take there? And do there?
- How can you start and finish your email?

5 Write your email (about 150–200 words). Make sure that you give your opinion about the place(s) you are talking about. Use Jake's email to help you.

LISTENING

1 📢43 **Listen to the conversations. Mark the sentences T (true) or F (false).**

CONVERSATION 1

0   The girl wants to go for a walk.   [F]

1   The girl doesn't know what a jigsaw puzzle is.   ☐

2   The girl doesn't want to do a jigsaw puzzle.   ☐

3   It's raining.   ☐

CONVERSATION 2

4   It's a cloudy day.   ☐

5   The boy doesn't want to wear trousers.   ☐

6   The boy likes the girl's T-shirt.   ☐

7   The girl doesn't understand what's written on her T-shirt.   ☐

2 📢43 **Listen again. Complete the lines from the conversations.**

CONVERSATION 1

BOY   0_____*What*_____ a horrible day today.

GIRL   Yes, it ¹_____.

BOY   I just thought, well, something different, you know, ²_____ a jigsaw puzzle.

GIRL   I know. What a ³_____ ! On a rainy day like today, it's a nice thing to do!

CONVERSATION 2

BOY   Wow, ⁴_____ fantastic day. It's so warm and ⁵_____ !

GIRL   So let's go out ⁶_____.

GIRL   Hey, nice ⁷_____. They look great.

BOY   Thanks. And I really like your T-shirt – ⁸_____ colour!

DIALOGUE

1 **Complete the conversation. Use the words in the list.**

~~can~~ | can't | idea | perhaps | maybe | let's

BOY   What a horrible day. It's cold and snowing.

GIRL   I know. What ⁰_____*can*_____ we do?

BOY   Well, we ¹_____ go outside. So, ²_____ do something here.

GIRL   Well, I thought, ³_____ we can watch a film.

BOY   Well, OK, yes. Or ⁴_____ we could play some computer games.

GIRL   That's a great ⁵_____.

2 **Write a conversation for the picture. Use Listening Exercise 2 and Dialogue Exercise 1 to help you.**

_____

_____

_____

_____

_____

_____

PHRASES FOR FLUENCY SB p.91

1 **Put the conversation in order.**

☐ A No problem. I'll call Jenny in a minute, she'll probably know.

☐ A Oh, yes, that's fixed it! Well done. Thank you!

[1] A Can you help me with my camera? Something's wrong with it and I don't know much about cameras.

☐ A Oh! So you can't help me, then?

☐ B Not really. I'm sorry.

☐ B Good idea. She's really good with these things. Oh – hang on! How about if you press this button here?

☐ B I don't know much either.

2 **Complete the conversation. Use the phrases in the list.**

~~in a minute~~ | not really | either | then | no problem

A (on the phone) Hi, John? Sorry, I'm a bit late. But I'll be at your place ⁰ _*in a minute*_ .

B ¹_____, Steve. Is there a lot of traffic, ²_____?

A ³_____. But I'm cycling and it's raining.

B Ugh. I hate cycling in the rain!

A I don't really like it ⁴_____. But I haven't got any money for the bus. Anyway, I shouldn't really be cycling and talking on the phone at the same time. So, bye!

Reading and Writing part 7

1   Complete the text. Write one word in each space.

My name **(0)**____*is*____ Alison Davey and I live **(1)**_____ Alice Springs, Australia. It's not a very big town – only about 25,000 people **(2)**_____ here.

Alice Springs (most people just call it 'Alice') is in the north **(3)**_____ the country. It's not a bad place to live **(4)**_____ it isn't very exciting. There's a nice park that you can visit and outside the town there are some mountains where you can **(5)**_____ walking.

It's a very hot place and it's very dry too because it doesn't **(6)**_____ very much.

In January, it's really hot and sometimes the **(7)**_____ can go up to 36 degrees. Alice is a very long **(8)**_____ from the sea so there aren't any beaches here.

Right now I'm at school but I want to go to university later. I want to go to Sydney because it's bigger **(9)**_____ Alice and a bit **(10)**_____ interesting too!

Exam guide: open cloze

In this kind of exercise, you have to write one word in each space. These exercises test your grammar and vocabulary, but mostly grammar.

- First, read the text from beginning to end without worrying about the spaces. Then you get a good idea of the overall meaning.
- Then, when you go back to the beginning, think about meaning and grammar – for example, in space number 1, you know that people live in a city or town, so the answer is *in*.

- Look at spaces 9 and 10 – what's the word that comes after a comparative adjective like *bigger*? And what's the word that goes before longer adjectives like *interesting*?
- Sometimes you have to think about meaning too. For example, in space 6, the text says that the town is very dry because something doesn't happen very much. What stops a place being dry? That's right – *rain*.

2   Complete the email. Write one word in each space.

Hi Amy,

Well, here we **(0)**____*are*____ at last. Niagara Falls! We flew from London **(1)**_____ Toronto and then **(2)**_____ dad hired a car and we drove to see the waterfalls. Wow – it's a fantastic place. I don't think there is anything more beautiful **(3)**_____ this in the world. I read that Niagara Falls isn't **(4)**_____ highest waterfall in the world – I think that's the Angel Falls in Venezuela – but it is really big. When you go close, the noise from the water is so loud, you can't **(5)**_____ other people talking!

We stayed for about two hours. We walked around and took a lot **(6)**_____ photos. Then we went to the hotel – it's a really small hotel **(7)**_____ only ten rooms. I'm happy because I've **(8)**_____ my own room, and my parents are in another room.

Well, we **(9)**_____ having a great time here. Tomorrow we go back to Toronto. Can I **(10)**_____ to you again from there?

See you!

Beth

10 AROUND TOWN

GRAMMAR

be going to for intentions `SB p.94`

1 ★☆☆ **Complete the sentences with the correct form of the verb *to be*. Use the contracted form.**

0 I _'m_ going to buy some stamps at the post office.

1 We _____ going to see a show at the concert hall.

2 I'm taking my children to the sports centre. They _____ going to have a swimming lesson.

3 I'm going to the shopping mall to meet my wife. She _____ going to take me for lunch.

4 We're going to the bus station. We _____ going to catch the number 51 home.

2 ★★☆ **Complete the questions, then match them with the answers. Use the verbs in brackets.**

0 _Are_ you going _to watch_ the game? (watch)

1 _____ they going _____ in a hotel? (stay)

2 _____ we going _____ Gran this weekend? (visit)

3 _____ Dave going _____ a taxi? (take)

4 _____ Jo going _____ the competition? (enter)

5 _____ Katie going _____ tonight? (cook)

a ☐ No, they're not. They're going camping.

b ☐ No, he's going to walk there.

c ☐ Yes, she is. She's going to win!

d ☐ I hope so. I'm so tired.

e ☐ *O* Yes, I am. I love football.

f ☐ Yes, we are. We're going to go on Sunday.

3 ★★☆ **Complete the answers with *going to* and the verbs in brackets.**

What ⁰ _are you going to do_ (do) when you leave school?

A 'I ¹_____ (study) Maths at Nottingham University. Two of my friends ²_____ (go) there too so we ³_____ (find) a house and live in it together.'

B 'I'm not sure. My best friend ⁴_____ (travel) around the world and he wants me to go with him. I ⁵_____ (not do) that – I haven't got enough money – but I ⁶_____ (not go) to university either.

4 ★★★ **Write five plans you have for this year. Use *going to*.**

I'm going to ... _____

_____

_____

_____

Present continuous for arrangements `SB p.95`

5 ★★☆ **Look at Claire's diary. Complete the sentences with the present continuous form of the verbs in brackets.**

	Morning	Afternoon	Evening
Monday		tennis – Sue	kids – cinema
Tuesday	breakfast with Tim		
Wednesday			party at Jo's
Thursday	meeting with Jen	dentist – 4 pm	
Friday	golf		fly to Rome

0 Claire and Sue _are playing_ (play) tennis on Monday afternoon.

1 Claire _____ (fly) to Rome on Friday evening.

2 Claire _____ (go) to Jo's party on Wednesday evening.

3 Claire _____ (go) to the dentist on Thursday afternoon.

4 Claire and Tim _____ (have) breakfast on Tuesday morning.

5 Claire _____ (play) golf on Friday morning.

6 Claire and her children _____ (go) to the cinema on Monday evening.

7 Claire and Jen _____ (have) a meeting on Thursday morning.

6 ★★★ Write the questions for the answers about Claire. Use the present continuous of the verbs.

0 *Is Claire going to the dentist on Thursday?*
   Yes, she is. Her appointment is at 4 pm.

1 _____
   No, they're having breakfast.

2 _____
   No, she's flying in the evening.

3 _____
   Yes, but they don't know what film to see yet.

4 _____
   That's right. They're playing in the afternoon.

7 ★★ Mark the sentences P (present arrangement) or F (future arrangement).

0 Henry's not at home. He's fishing with his dad. **P**
1 Sorry, I can't help you. I'm studying. ☐
2 Are you doing anything this evening? ☐
3 Look at the baby! She's trying to walk. ☐
4 Is Aunt Mary coming to stay next week? ☐
5 We're looking at new houses this afternoon. ☐
6 I'm staying at my friend's house tonight. ☐

8 ★★★ Write five arrangements you have for this weekend. Use the present continuous.

Adverbs SB p.97

9 ★ ☆ ☆ Read the sentences. Write the names under the pictures.

Bella paints really well.
Molly paints quite badly.
Tim rides his bike dangerously.
Ben rides his bike carefully.

0 *Molly* _____ **1** _____

2 _____ **3** _____

10 ★★ ☆ Unscramble the words to make adjectives. Then write the adverb form.

		adjective	adverb
0	saye	*easy*	*easily*
1	wols		
2	kiquc		
3	souranged		
4	revosun		
5	teiqu		
6	dab		
7	larefuc		
8	dogo		

11 ★★★ Circle the correct words.

0 Jackson played very *good /* well *,* and won the match *easy /* easily *.*

1 It was an *easy / easily* test and I finished it really *quick / quickly.*

2 My dad isn't a very *careful / carefully* driver and sometimes he drives quite *dangerous / dangerously.*

3 Please be *quiet / quietly* in the library – you can talk, but not too *loud / loudly.*

4 I didn't do *good / well* in the test – I had a really *bad / badly* day.

5 He's quite a *nervous / nervously* person and he talks really *quiet / quietly.*

GET IT RIGHT! 👁

Adverbs usually come immediately after the object of the sentence or after the verb (if there is no object). They never come between the verb and the object.

✓ He drives his car dangerously.
✗ He drives dangerously his car.

Change the adjective in brackets into an adverb and put it in the correct place in the sentence.

0 He can run fast, but he can't swim. (good)
   He can run fast, but he can't swim well.

1 You should drive when it's raining. (careful)
   _____

2 She speaks French and German. (fluent)
   _____

3 She was walking because she was late for school. (quick)
   _____

4 They did the homework because they worked together. (easy)
   _____

VOCABULARY

Places in town

- bus station
- concert hall
- football stadium
- car park
- police station
- opera house
- shopping mall
- post office
- harbour
- sports centre
- skyscraper
- castle

Things in a town

zebra crossing

youth club

speed camera

graffiti wall

cycle lane

litter bin

billboard

high street

skateboard park

Key words in context

culture	I love meeting people from different **cultures** – there's so much you can learn from them.
population	The **population** of our town is about 20,000.
local	Our **local** shop is just across the road from our house.
invite	The Jacksons **invited** us to dinner at their house.
tourism	**Tourism** is very important for our country. Millions of people visit us each year.
pedestrian	**Pedestrians** must be careful when they cross the road.
fluent	He speaks really good French. He's almost **fluent**.
tourist attraction	The museum is a really big **tourist attraction**. Lots of people visit it.
sand	We went to the beach and now I've got **sand** in my hair.
mine	This **mine** goes more than 200 m under the ground.
diamond	Is that a **diamond** ring? Wow, it's beautiful.
resort	Cannes is a popular **resort** in the south of France.
demolish	They **demolished** the old stadium because they want to build a new one.

Places in a town [SB p.94]

1 ★☆☆ **Complete the words. Use the picture clues to help you.**

0 concert hall

1 b _ s st _ t _ _ n

2 f _ _ tb _ ll
st _ d _ _ m

3 c _ r p _ rk

4 p _ l _ c _
st _ t _ _ n

5 p _ st _ ff _ c _

6 sp _ rts c _ ntr _

2 ★★☆ **Complete the text. Use the words in Exercise 1.**

Our town is great. It's got everything I need. There's a really good sports ⁰ _centre_ . You can do lots of different sports. There's a big ¹_____ hall as well and I often go to see my favourite bands there. Most Saturdays I go to the football ²_____ to see our football team play. There's a really big shopping ³_____ with lots of shops in it. And if you ever get bored, you can go to the bus ⁴_____ to catch a bus and visit another town.

3 ★★★ **Where are these people? Choose from the places in Exercise 1.**

0 'What time does the swimming pool close?'
sports centre

1 'I want to send this letter to Australia.' _____

2 'I think Manchester United are going to win today.'
_____

3 'What time is the next bus to Liverpool?'
_____

4 'I want to buy some new shoes.' _____

5 'The band start playing at 8 pm.' _____

6 'It costs £2 every hour we stay.' _____

7 'There's a problem at the bank. Come quickly.'
_____

Things in town [SB p.97]

4 ★☆☆ **Write compound nouns using the nouns in the lists.**

~~cycle~~ | graffiti | speed | zebra | bill | litter
~~lane~~ | board | camera | crossing | bin | wall

0 _cycle lane_   3 _____

1 _____   4 _____

2 _____   5 _____

5 ★★☆ **Match the words from Exercises 1 and 4 to the definitions.**

0 Cars slow down for this. _speed camera_

1 You find lots of shops here. _____

2 You can ride your bike safely here. _____

3 It advertises things on the side of the road.
_____

4 Use this to cross the road safely. _____

5 A great place for local artists to paint. _____

6 A good place for young people to meet and have fun. _____

7 Throw your rubbish in this. _____

6 ★★★ **Which of these sentences are true about your town? Correct the ones that are false.**

1 Cars always stop at zebra crossings.

2 There are lots of things for young people to do. There are graffiti walls and a really good youth club.

3 Speed cameras make the roads safer.

4 You can get everywhere on your bike using cycle lanes.

5 People always use the litter bins to throw away rubbish.

6 There are lots of billboards.

7 The high street is full of shoppers at the weekend.

READING

1 [REMEMBER AND CHECK] **What are these things? Check your answers in the blogs on page 93 of the Student's Book.**

0 The Burj al Arab
   A building in Dubai that looks like a ship's sail.

1 Jebel Ali
   _____

2 khaliji
   _____

3 Yellowknife
   _____

4 Snowking Winter Festival
   _____

2 **Read the article. Write the names of the towns under the pictures.**

1 _____

2 _____

3 _____

4 _____

UNUSUAL TOWNS

Monowi, USA

Elsie Eiler is famous in the town of Monowi in Nebraska and everybody knows her name. That's because Elsie is the only person who lives there. Monowi was never a big town. In the 1930s the population was 150 but over the years people slowly started leaving. In 2000 there were only two people left; Elsie and her husband, Rudy. When Rudy died, Elsie became the only citizen.

Thames Town, China

Shanghai is one of China's biggest cities. But just outside of Shanghai is a rather unusual town called Thames Town. It cost £500 million to build and it is part of their 'One City, Nine Towns' project. When you walk down the streets there you might forget you are in China. You might start thinking you are in England.

That is because Thames Town is a copy of an English town. The streets and the buildings all look English. It has red phone boxes, London street signs, fish and chip shops and English pubs. There are also statues of Harry Potter and James Bond. Elsewhere in China, you can find the Eiffel Tower, an Austrian village and even Stonehenge.

Sheffield, Australia

In the 1980s, the citizens of Sheffield on the Australian island of Tasmania decided they wanted more tourists to visit their town. They had an idea to turn their streets into an outdoor art gallery. They asked artists to paint huge paintings on the walls around town. Children from the local school helped too. They painted little murals on the rubbish bins. There are now more than 60 of these murals, which show important scenes from history.

The plan worked and these days about 200,000 people visit Sheffield every year.

Roswell, USA

Some people believe that in 1947 an alien spacecraft crashed near the town of Roswell in New Mexico. They believe that the American military seized this UFO and took it to a secret place outside of the town. These days Roswell sees many tourists who are interested in life on other planets. There are many shops that sell souvenirs and there is one fast food restaurant with a UFO theme. There is also a museum about aliens.

3 **Read the article again. Write the names of the towns after the sentences.**

0 Are there aliens here? *Roswell* _____

1 They wanted more people to visit here. _____

2 It has a population of one. _____

3 It's near to a really big city. _____

4 People didn't want to live here. _____

5 It's like being in another country. _____

6 It's a mysterious place. _____

7 It's a great place if you like art. _____

DEVELOPING WRITING

An informal letter / email

Hi Jessie,

Thanks for your letter and all your news. Sorry about your broken arm – what a terrible thing to happen. I hope you feel better soon. Just be careful when you get back on your bike!

Anyway, I'm sorry my reply is a bit late, but there's so much happening it's difficult to find any free time.

The move here was OK. The new house is nice and big. I've finally got my own bedroom. Worcester is quite a small town (well, compared to Manchester) but it seems quite nice. There are lots of good shops on the High Street and there are a few parks to hang out in. I'm sending you a photo of the cathedral. It's a really beautiful building. I'm spending most of my time at the sports centre. I'm quite fit at the moment. I haven't got any friends here yet but I'm starting school on Monday. I'm sure I'll find some. I'm feeling a bit nervous.

Anyway, I miss you loads, of course. I can't wait to hear all your news. Please give my love to everyone, especially Tom and Jasmine. By the way, Mum says we're going to visit next month so I hope I'll see you all soon. Hope everything's OK.

Lots of love,

Olivia

1   Read the email. Answer the questions.

0   How did Jessie break her arm?
     She fell off her bike.

1   Where is Olivia living now?
     _____

2   Where did she live?
     _____

3   How does Olivia feel about starting school?
     _____

2   Read the email again. Write the expressions that mean:

1   I was sad to hear about …
     _____

2   I think about you a lot.
     _____

3   Please write to me soon.
     _____

4   Say hello to …
     _____

Writing tip: an informal letter / email

We usually write informal letters to family and friends to keep in touch and pass on our news. These days most people do this with emails.

- Use informal, friendly language.
- If you are writing a reply to a letter, don't forget to react to your friend's news. We usually do this in our opening paragraph.
- Always ask how the person you are writing to is. You can do this at the beginning or the end of your letter.
- Use the main paragraph of the letter to give your news.

3   Write an informal letter to a friend (about 120–150 words). Choose one of these situations.

- Your pen friend wants to know more about the town where you live. Write and tell them.
- You're going to move house. Write to your friend to give them the news and tell them a bit about the town.
- You are spending the holiday with your aunt and uncle. Write to your friend and tell them about the town where you are staying.

LISTENING

1 🔊44 **Listen to the conversations. Complete the table.**

	Invitation accepted	Invitation not accepted
Conversation 1	☐	☐
Conversation 2	☐	☐
Conversation 3	☐	☐

2 🔊44 **Listen again. Complete the sentences.**

Kate and Jim

Kate invites Jim to ⁰ *the sports centre* .
He says ¹_____ because
²_____ .

Ian and Ruth

Ian invites Ruth to ³_____ on
⁴_____ .
She offers to pay for ⁵_____ .
He says the tickets are ⁶_____ .

Dan and Anna

Dan invites Anna to ⁷_____ at
⁸_____ .
She is ⁹_____ until
¹⁰_____ .
They arrange to meet ¹¹_____ .

DIALOGUE

1 🔊44 **Put the first two conversations in order. Then listen again and check.**

1	**1**	KATE	Do you want to go to the sports centre later?
	☐	KATE	OK, maybe next week then.
	☐	KATE	What about tomorrow?
	☐	JIM	No, I'm busy all week.
	☐	JIM	Let's see.
	☐	JIM	I'm sorry. I can't. I'm busy.
2	☐	IAN	It's *Madam Butterfly*. I've got tickets right at the front.
	☐	IAN	No, it's a present from me.
	☐	IAN	Well, you deserve it.
	☐	IAN	Would you like to go to the opera house with me on Saturday?
	☐	RUTH	That would be great. What's the opera?
	☐	RUTH	Wow. How much were they? You must let me pay for mine.
	☐	RUTH	That's really kind of you.

2 **Write two short conversations. Use these situations.**

Conversation 1
- Boy invites girl to cinema.
- She says yes.
- They agree on a time.

Conversation 2
- Girl invites boy to party.
- He asks what day and when.
- He can't make it and says why.

▮▮▮ TRAIN TO THiNK ▮▮▮

Problem solving

1 **The town council has money to build one new building. Look at the first three suggestions and match the advantages and disadvantages to each one.**

~~good to get bands into town~~
bad for shops on high street
create lots of jobs
stop people parking on street
could bring more cars into town
could be noisy at night

Suggestions	Advantages	Disadvantages
concert hall	*good to get bands into town*	
shopping mall		
car park		

2 **Think of an advantage and a disadvantage for these three suggestions.**

Suggestions	Advantages	Disadvantages
football stadium		
bus station		
sports centre		

3 **Complete the statement. Use your own ideas.**

I think the _____ is the best idea
because _____
and _____ .

Pronunciation

Voiced /ð/ and unvoiced /θ/ consonants
Go to page 121. 🔊

Reading and Writing part 4

1   Read the article about Shanghai. Are sentences 1–4 'Right' (A) or 'Wrong' (B)? If there isn't enough information to answer 'Right' or 'Wrong', choose 'Doesn't say' (C).

Mini-Shanghai

It's difficult to know exactly how many people live in the Chinese city of Shanghai, but it's at least 20 million. For sure, it's one of the world's biggest cities. Of course, you need a lot of space to find room for so many people, and to give you an idea of just how big Shanghai is, there is a model of the whole city on the third floor of Shanghai's Urban Planning

Museum. The model is huge. It's 93 m² and it covers the whole floor of the museum. In fact, it's too big to take a photograph of the whole thing. You can try but you'll find you have to take quite a few photos.

Of course, Shanghai is a city that is growing fast and every year there are about 200 new skyscrapers. The model does not show what Shanghai looks like now. It shows Shanghai in the year 2020.

0   The population of Shanghai is more than 20 million.
   (A) Right   B Wrong   C Doesn't say

1   The model is on the top floor of the museum.
   A Right   B Wrong   C Doesn't say

2   You are not allowed to take photos of the model.
   A Right   B Wrong   C Doesn't say

3   The model shows Shanghai in the future.
   A Right   B Wrong   C Doesn't say

4   The model city is a popular tourist attraction.
   A Right   B Wrong   C Doesn't say

Exam guide: right, wrong or doesn't say

In the KEY Reading and Writing part 4 you must read a text and then decide if the information in some sentences about the text is right or wrong. Sometimes there isn't enough information to decide, and for these sentences you should choose the 'Doesn't say' option.

- Read through the text quickly to get an idea of what it is about. Then read a second time, more slowly.
- Read through the questions. Can you answer any of them immediately? Check in the text to make sure you have the correct answer.
- For each question, find the part of the text it refers to. Use the key words in the question to help you find the correct part of the text. For example, in question 0 the words 20 million are there in the first sentence of the text. This is the part of the text you need to look at.

- If you can't find any information to decide if the question is right or wrong, this probably means the text 'doesn't say'. For example, question 1 says the model is on the top floor of the museum. In the text it says it's on the third floor. We don't know how many floors the museum has. The third floor might be the top floor but we can't be sure. We have to choose the 'Doesn't say' option here.
- The order of the questions is the same as the order of the information in the text.

2   Read Jenny's article about moving home. Are sentences 1–5 'Right' (A) or 'Wrong' (B)? If there isn't enough information to answer 'Right' or 'Wrong', choose 'Doesn't say' (C).

A move to the countryside

For the first twelve years of my life my family lived in a large city. Two years ago my parents decided to move to the countryside. I was horrified. How could I leave all my friends? How could I live somewhere with no cinema, with no skateboard park, where the nearest shop was more than 3 km away?

But Mum and Dad didn't listen to me. They were tired of the city life. Mum's a writer so she can live anywhere and Dad looks after me and my two younger brothers. They thought the country was a better place to bring up children.

Well, two years later and I agree with them. I love it here. I love the freedom of being outside. You can ride your bike everywhere. You don't have to worry about cars. Of course, I found new friends. Not as many as I had, but that isn't a problem. I'm still in contact with my very best friend from the city, Anna, and she comes to visit most holidays. She loves it here. She wants her parents to move too.

0   Jenny is 13 years old.
   A Right   (B) Wrong   C Doesn't say

1   Jenny wasn't happy with the idea of moving to the countryside.
   A Right   B Wrong   C Doesn't say

2   Jenny's mum works for a newspaper.
   A Right   B Wrong   C Doesn't say

3   There are five people in Jenny's family.
   A Right   B Wrong   C Doesn't say

4   Jenny has got more friends now.
   A Right   B Wrong   C Doesn't say

5   Jenny went to school with Anna when she lived in the city.
   A Right   B Wrong   C Doesn't say

CONSOLIDATION

LISTENING

1 🔊**46** **Listen to the conversations. Circle A, B or C.**

1 What kind of holiday is Emma going to suggest to her parents?

   A hotel   **B** houseboat   **C** camping

2 Who's got the best idea about what they can do?

   A Mike   **B** Dad   **C** Mum

3 When are Emma and her family going on holiday?

   A 4 July   **B** 18 July   **C** 8 August

2 🔊**46** **Listen again. Answer the questions.**

0 Why don't Mike and Emma want to go to the same hotel as last year?

   They think it would be boring.

1 What does Emma think about a camping holiday?

   _____

2 What does Dad think about Emma's suggestion of a holiday on a houseboat?

   _____

3 What is Mum going to suggest to her and her husband's parents?

   _____

4 Mum makes a joke. What does she say?

   _____

5 How soon are Emma and her family going on their holiday?

   _____

VOCABULARY

3 **Circle the correct words.**

Before you go on a holiday, you need to think carefully about where you want to go. If you decide to go to a place in the ⁰*mountains* / *beach*, for example, you have to know that the weather can be ¹*freezing* / *hot* (even in summer), and it can also be quite ²*windy* / *warm*.

Everybody knows that deserts have ³*dry* / *wet* weather, but people sometimes forget that a ⁴*beach* / *forest* holiday means you are close to a lot of water, so the air can be quite ⁵*dry* / *humid*. During the summer months, this can mean that it can get too ⁶*hot* / *cold*, and not everybody likes that. Here are my family's plans for our next holiday: First we're going to ⁷*spend* / *spending* two weeks at a ⁸*hill* / *lake*. Then, on the 1 September, we are ⁹*leaving* / *leave* for a weekend in the mountains.

4 Complete the sentences. Use the words in the list.

~~concert hall~~ | post office | cycle lane | billboards
litter bin | speed camera | zebra crossing

0 I can't believe we can't get tickets for the show. There's room for 2,000 people in the *concert hall*.

1 I need some stamps. Can you go to the _____ for me?

2 Careful – don't drive so fast! There's a _____ ahead, so keep to 50 kph, OK?

3 I want to throw this paper away. Is there a _____ around here?

4 Did you see that driver?! There was someone on the _____ and he didn't stop!

5 There's a new _____ that goes along the beach! It's great – we ride along it on Sundays.

6 He's a professional photographer. His photos are on all the _____ at the moment.

GRAMMAR

5 **Circle the correct words.**

LILY   When are you going on holiday?

OLIVER   Next weekend. And we are all looking forward to it. It's going to be the ⁰*more* / *most* relaxing time of the year!

LILY   That place on the coast where you are staying, is it ¹*hotter* / *hottest* than it is here?

OLIVER   Not really. It's ²*more cold* / *colder* than it is here, and there's usually ³*more* / *most* wind. So the temperature is normally five or six degrees lower ⁴*more* / *than* here.

LILY   And it's the world's ⁵*more* / *most* attractive coast.

OLIVER   Do you think so? Well, it's ⁶*more* / *most* beautiful than other places, but we can't swim in the ocean.

LILY   Can't you?

OLIVER   No, the water temperature is just too cold. And I don't think it's ⁷*safe* / *safely*.

LILY   Oh, really. Are there any ⁸*dangerous* / *dangerously* fish?

OLIVER   I don't think there are. But the waves are really high because of the wind. You'd need to swim really ⁹*good* / *well* to go in. But then you'd come out ¹⁰*quick* / *quickly* again.

DIALOGUE

6 **Complete the conversation. Use the phrases in the list.**

~~going to go~~ | going to come | can't go | I'd
no problem | like to | busy with | be with me
are going to | you like to

EVA Jack, I'm ^{0} *going to go* to the concert on
Saturday. Would ^{1}_____ come along?
My friend Nick ^{2}_____, so I've got a
ticket if you want it.

JACK Saturday? I'm sorry, I can't. I'm ^{3}_____
a project.

EVA I see. Well, maybe another time.

JACK Yeah, thanks for asking. Oh, would you and
Nick ^{4}_____ come over to our place
next Sunday, maybe? We can sit in the garden,
and enjoy the beautiful weather. Gavin and
Claire ^{5}_____ come too.

EVA ^{6}_____ love to. That would be great.
Let me talk to Nick. I know he's going to visit
some relatives on Saturday, but I think he's
^{7}_____ back on Sunday morning. So it
should be fine. Can I tell you this evening?

JACK ^{8}_____. Talk to Nick first, and give me
a ring any time.

(later, on the phone)

JACK Hello?

EVA Oh, hi, Jack. It's about next Sunday. I'm really
sorry. Nick won't ^{9}_____ on Sunday.
He's coming back after 7 in the evening, so I'm
going to come alone.

JACK OK.

READING

7 **Read the magazine article about Peru. Circle the
correct endings (A or B) for each sentence.**

0 Peru is a very popular holiday place …

   (A) because it offers tourists a lot of attractions.

   B but the weather is often not very good.

1 A holiday on the coast in summer is good …

   A if you like hot and dry weather.

   B if you don't mind a lot of foggy and rainy days.

2 In the Andes, in winter …

   A it's usually foggy, and not very cold.

   B it's usually dry, and it can be very, very cold.

3 In the east of the country there are no mountains …

   A and the weather doesn't change much
throughout the year.

   B and there are extreme differences between
summer and winter.

So many kinds of weather!

Peru isn't just a beautiful country. Tourists love
it because of its attractive jungles, its stunning
beaches and the fantastic Peruvian food. And many
people come to see Machu Picchu, a very interesting
Inca site that's more than 500 years old. But Peru is
also famous for its many different climates. If you
travel from one place to another, you can have very
different weather on the same day!

The weather on the coast is usually dry and warm,
often hot. In the summer, it's hardly ever rainy there.
In winter, the coast is often foggy, and the fog even
has its own name, *garúa*. In the areas near the ocean,
the so-called 'rainy season' starts around late May
and comes to an end in October.

In the mountains, the famous Andes, it's often cool,
and sometimes cold. The summers there are usually
rainy, but the winters are very dry, and can be
freezing. In the east, where there are no mountains,
the weather is usually hot and humid all year round.

WRITING

8 **Write a paragraph about the weather in your
country (about 80–100 words). Think about
these questions.**

- Is the weather the same all over the country, or are
there differences?

- If the weather is different, can you say why?

- What times of the year are good for tourists who
want to visit your country?

GRAMMAR

will / won't for future predictions SB p.104

1 ★☆☆ **Put the words in order to make sentences.**

0 'll / home / by / I / 7.30. / be
   I'll be home by 7.30.

1 Sunday / home / and / we / stay / at / relax. / On / 'll
   _____

2 come round / you / to / place / Will / tomorrow? / my
   _____

3 you? / I / to / know / where / find / Will
   _____

4 come / the / party. / to / won't / Sebastian
   _____

2 ★★☆ **Complete the sentences. Use the *will* future form of the verbs. Then match sentences 1–5 to sentences a–f.**

0 [e] Don't worry. I'm sure you *won't have* problems with the test. (not have)

1 [ ] This year at school _____ cool. (be)

2 [ ] I'm not sure a picnic is such a great idea.

3 [ ] Kate's not sure if she _____ to the cinema tonight. (go)

4 [ ] Ben and Mason _____ back from their trip soon. (be)

5 [ ] Don't try to repair your bike without me.

a Our teachers _____ probably _____ us to a youth camp in the last week before the holidays. (take)

b Perhaps she _____ at home and work on her project. (stay)

c It _____ probably _____ raining later today. (start)

d I'm sure they _____ lots of stories to tell. (have)

e You always study hard.

f We _____ it together. (do) That _____ much more fun. (be)

3 ★★☆ **Complete the questions. Use the *will* future form of the verbs in the list.**

~~learn~~ | get married | have | go | have | live

0 When __*will*__ you __*learn*__ to drive?

1 _____ you ever _____ in another country?

2 _____ you ever _____ a sports car?

3 How many children _____ you _____?

4 When do you think you _____?

5 _____ you _____ to university after school?

4 ★★★ **Complete the answers. Use the *will* future form of the verbs in the list. Then match them with the questions in Exercise 3.**

~~have~~ | drive | live | get | take | do

0 I __*'ll have*__ lots. I love children. [3]

1 I think I _____ in Japan for a year before I go to university. [ ]

2 A sports car? No. I don't think I _____ ever even _____ a car. [ ]

3 I think _____ the driving test before I go to university. [ ]

4 I really don't know but I'm sure I _____ married for a long time. [ ]

5 Yes, I think I _____ that but I'm not sure what I want to study yet. [ ]

5 ★★★ **Answer the questions from Exercise 3 so they are true for you. Use the *will* future form of the verbs.**

_____
_____
_____
_____
_____
_____

Pronunciation

The /h/ consonant sound

Go to page 121.

First conditional `SB p.106`

6 ★☆☆　Match each picture with two sentences.

0 I won't have a lot of money left if I buy it.	**B**
1 If he isn't careful, he'll break them.	
2 The neighbours will get angry if he doesn't stop.	
3 If I buy one of those, I won't be hungry any more.	
4 If he doesn't get up now, he'll be late for school.	
5 If he doesn't practise, he'll never play in a band.	

7 ★★☆　Complete the sentences. Circle the most likely options.

0 He won't pass the test
- (a) if he doesn't study hard.
- b if he studies hard.

1 I'm sure all of your friends will come to your party
- a if you don't invite them.
- b if you invite them.

2 It's raining. If you don't put on your hat,
- a you'll get wet.
- b you won't get wet.

3 She'll book a trip to Rome
- a if it isn't too expensive.
- b if it's too expensive.

4 If we don't play better,
- a we'll win the match.
- b we'll lose the match.

5 If I find another of those T-shirts,
- a I won't get one for you.
- b I'll get one for you.

8 ★★☆　Complete the sentences. Use the first conditional form of the verbs in brackets.

0 If you _don't listen_ (not listen), your teacher _won't tell_ (not tell) you what to do again.

1 If we _____ (not feed) the cat, she _____ (be) very hungry.

2 The police _____ (stop) him if he _____ (not slow down).

3 If we _____ (take) a map with us, we _____ (find) the way home.

4 Nobody _____ (like) them if they _____ (behave) like that.

5 If Susie _____ (not help) me, I _____ (be) in trouble.

9 ★★★　Complete the sentences. Use what you think might be the consequences of these situations.

50 years from now …

1 If scientists invent cars that run without petrol, _____.

2 If time travel becomes possible, _____.

3 If there are 10 billion people on earth, _____.

4 If computers can speak all languages, _____.

5 If people can fly to Mars in 24 hours, _____.

Time clauses with *when / as soon as* `SB p.107`

10 ★★★　Read the sentences. Circle the correct words.

0 When we *arrive* / *'ll arrive*, we *send* / *'ll send* you a text message.

1 He *look* / *'ll look* for the book as soon as he *'s* / *'ll be* home.

2 We *watch* / *'ll watch* the film as soon as the electricity *comes* / *will come* back on.

3 As soon I *get* / *'ll get* the money, I *pay* / *'ll pay* you back.

4 I *take* / *'ll take* you to the new museum when you *come* / *'ll come* and see us.

5 Dad *returns* / *will return* from the US as soon as his job there *is* / *will be* finished.

GET IT RIGHT!
First conditional

We use the present simple in the *if* clause and *will* / *won't* in the <u>result</u> clause. We never use *will* / *won't* in the *if* clause.

✓ *If I see Rory, I'll tell him the news.*

✗ *If I will see Rory, I'll tell him the news.*

Find four incorrect uses of *will*. Correct them.

I don't know what to do! I feel ill, but if I won't go to school tomorrow, I'll miss the test. If I'll miss the test, I'll have to do it in the holidays. But if I will go to school and do the test when I'm ill, I'm sure I won't get a good mark. I won't be able to go to London in the holiday if I will have to do the test then. What a difficult decision!

VOCABULARY

Parts of the body

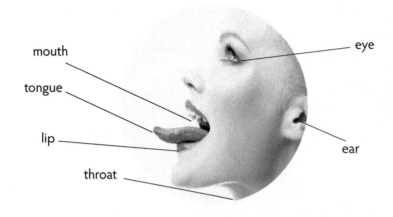

mouth
tongue
lip
throat
eye
ear

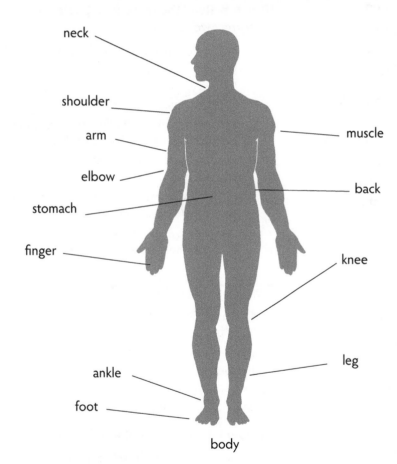

neck
shoulder
arm
elbow
stomach
finger
ankle
foot
muscle
back
knee
leg
body

Aches

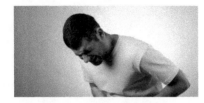

stomach ache

ear ache

headache

toothache

when / if

When we arrive, John will prepare some food. (It is certain we will arrive.)

If we arrive before 10, John will prepare some food. (It isn't certain we will arrive before 10.)

Key words in context

fresh air	Let's go outside. I need a bit of **fresh air**.
keep fit	She runs three times a week to **keep fit**.
hurt	Careful! You could **hurt** yourself.
fall	Thomas had a very bad **fall**. He fell down the stairs.
break a leg	I **broke a leg** when I was ten.
see in the dark	I can't **see very well in the dark** so I don't drive at night.
stressed	He seems a bit **stressed**. He's usually not so nervous.
shout at someone	Don't **shout at me**. It wasn't my fault.

Expressions with *do*

do exercise
do the cleaning
do the cooking
do homework
do OK
do well
do (food / drink, in a café, restaurant, etc.)
do (12 kilometres to the litre)

Parts of the body SB p.104

1 ★☆☆ **Unscramble the words to make parts of the body.**

~~alenk~~ | bolwe | ilp | elusmc
asmotch | tatroh | enek

0   _ankle_

1   _____

2   _____

3   _____

4   _____

5   _____

6   _____

2 ★★☆ **Complete the sentences. Use words for parts of the body.**

0   When he tried to put his shoe on his f _oot_ , he noticed that his a _nkle_ hurt.

1   This rucksack is so heavy that all the m_____ in my n_____ and my s_____ hurt.

2   I've got a lot of pain all up my left arm. It hurts from the ends of my f_____, through my h_____, and up to my e_____.

3   I walked straight into a window. My whole face really hurts; my l_____, my m_____, my e_____ and my e_____ – they all hurt!

4   I ate too much. I've got a s_____ ache.

3 ★★☆ **Write verbs or phrases that match the parts of the body. How many can you find?**

foot – _run, walk,_____

mouth – _eat,_____

ear – _listen to music,_____

arm – _____

eye – _____

fingers – _____

tongue – _____

when and *if* SB p.107

4 ★☆☆ (Circle) **the correct words.**

0   Mum doesn't know when she'll be back. She'll phone us (*if*) / *when* she has to work late.

1   I can't do that now. I'll try to do it tomorrow *if* / *when* I've got time.

2   I'm not sure where my camera is right now. I'll give it to you *if* / *when* I find it.

3   It's still dark outside. We'll start in an hour, *if* / *when* it's light.

4   It's Jane's birthday on Sunday. She'll be sad *if* / *when* you don't give her a present.

5   I'm writing the email now. I'll be with you in a few minutes *if* / *when* I finish.

WordWise SB p.109
Expressions with *do*

5 ★☆☆ **Match the sentences with the pictures.**

0   Let's go in there. They do great food. `e`

1   I'm happy to do the cooking, but it seems we need to go shopping first. ☐

2   I think we need to do some cleaning here. ☐

3   This has the latest technology. It does 30 kilometres to the litre. ☐

4   And Dad thinks I'm doing my homework. Ha ha ha! ☐

5   He isn't doing very well at the moment. I don't think he can give a speech today. ☐

6 ★★☆ **Complete the questions. Use the words in the list.**

~~exercise~~ | ice cream | well | cooking | homework

0   A   How often do you do _exercise_ in a week?

    B   I run on Mondays and Wednesdays, and go to the gym on Fridays.

1   A   Did you do _____ in your last English test?

    B   Yes, I got top marks.

2   A   Who does the _____ in your family?

    B   My dad. He loves it. He thinks he's a chef.

3   A   Who does the best _____ in your town?

    B   There's an Italian place on my street. It's wonderful.

4   A   When do you usually do your _____?

    B   Straight after school, when I can still remember everything.

7 ★★★ **Answer the questions in Exercise 6 so they are true for you.**

READING

1 REMEMBER AND CHECK **Complete the sentences. Check your answers in the article on page 103 of the Student's Book.**

0 Because of the food we eat, we'll probably be _taller_ in the future.

1 If we continue doing less physical work, our _____ will get _____.

2 We can expect our legs to get _____, our feet to get _____, and our fingers to get _____.

3 We'll do a lot of computer work, for which we need our eyes and our fingers, so we can expect that both will get _____.

4 Experts think that our _____ will get smaller because we won't talk so much.

5 They also say that our little toe will _____.

6 In the future, we'll grow less _____.

2 **Read the text quickly. Which of these inventions produces electricity, and where does the energy come from?**

It's the _____. The energy comes from _____.

3 **Read the text again. Are sentences 1–5 'Right' (A)** ✳ **or 'Wrong' (B)? If there isn't enough information to answer 'Right' or 'Wrong', choose 'Doesn't say' (C).**

0 If you have the Things Spotter you'll never lose things again.   A   B   Ⓒ

1 The Things Spotter won't be very expensive.   A   B   C

2 The Fire Recharger turns solar energy into flames.   A   B   C

3 The Fire Recharger will be good to have when there is no electricity.   A   B   C

4 DigiGoggles will make scuba diving easier.   A   B   C

5 People will be able to use DigiGoogles for surfing the web.   A   B   C

The future of ...

Losing things ... and finding them again!

If you are one of those people who often lose things, you'll be happy with an invention that will soon become very popular – or so experts think. The Things Spotter will allow you to find everything, from your wallet to your cat. It'll look like a small key tag that you can put on your wallet or your cat, and it won't cost a lot. The tag will be connected to your mobile phone via BlueTooth technology. When you lose something, you'll press a button on your mobile and a map on your screen will tell you where to look.

Charging your phone in the wilderness

Imagine going camping in the wilderness. You have no electricity, and you need to make an urgent phone call. The batteries on your mobile are empty. Some engineers are working on a Fire Recharger. It turns heat from fire into electricity. This means you will be able to charge your empty batteries if you use a small gas fire, or even a wood campfire. When this gadget is in the shops, it'll be good to have at home too. It'll help people to stay in contact, even if there are power cuts, for example because of heavy storms.

Underwater photography

Don't you love them too – those colourful underwater photos of tropical fish and coral reefs? But these photos are not easy to take. Underwater photography is an expensive hobby, and good equipment is also very, very heavy. But heavy underwater cameras will soon be a thing of the past. Maybe in a few years' time you will buy a pair of DigiGoggles before you go on holiday. That's the name of a special diving mask that can take photos too. And you probably won't even have to press a button to get a good shot. Open and close your eyes twice and your camera will go 'click'!

DEVELOPING WRITING

Taking phone messages

1 🔊48 **Listen to the conversation. Why can't Neil take the call?** (Circle) **the correct answer.**

   A   He's having lunch.

   B   He's out shopping.

   C   He's in a meeting.

2 🔊48 **Listen again. Read the secretary's message for Neil. Which two pieces of information in the message are wrong?**

   1   _____

   2   _____

> To: Neil
>
> Tim called. He says he booked a taxi for 7 o'clock tomorrow morning. The driver thinks it'll take two hours to get to the airport. Tim says there's enough time to meet the TV people after the flight. You can reach him on his mobile. I've got a doctor's appointment now. I'll be back shortly after 4. Please text me if anything's not clear.
>
> Best,
> Grace

3 **Grace wrote another phone message on the same day. Read it. Then answer the questions.**

> Isaac,
>
> Just got home after busy day. Samuel's mum phoned. Told me Maths test didn't go well. She says no pocket money for Samuel for two weeks. We need to talk, too. Off to gym now. Back 9.30. See you then.
>
> Love (worried),
> Mum

   1   Which of the two messages is formal?

      A   the message to Neil   B   the message to Isaac

   2   Write the names of the people she writes to.

      She finishes the message to ¹_____ in a formal way.

      She finishes the message to ²_____ in an informal way.

      In the message to ³_____ she writes full sentences.

      In the message to ⁴_____ she leaves out certain words.

4 **Grace left these words out in her message to Isaac. Where could they go? Rewrite the message in your notebooks.**

a | the | I | she | there's
I'm | the | at | I'll be | I'll

Writing tip: taking a phone message

Listen carefully and make notes about the most important information. Write down key words:

- Who phoned?
- Who is the message for?
- What is the message?
- What's the caller's phone number / email?

After the phone call, write out the message. You can leave out words that are not so important in informal messages – but only if the message is still clear:

- personal pronouns: *I, we, he, she,* etc.
- prepositions: *to, at, on, in,* etc.
- auxiliary verbs: *is, am, are,* etc.
- articles: *the, a, an*

5 **Read the note. Cross out all the words that can be left out.**

> Hi Sandy,
>
> Thomas called. He wanted to ask you about the French homework. There are a few things he doesn't understand. Also he wants to go and see a film tonight. Are you interested? Can you please call him back? His new mobile number is 87964 0360.
>
> Leah

6 🔊49 **Listen to the conversations. Take the messages the callers want to leave.**

- Decide whether the message is formal or informal.
- Make sure you include the most important information.
- When your message is finished, read it again. Ask yourself, 'Will the message be clear to the person who it is for?'

> MESSAGE FROM: _____
>
> MESSAGE FOR: _____
>
> MESSAGE: _____
>
> _____
>
> _____
>
> _____
>
> CONTACT DETAILS: _____

LISTENING

1 🔊50 Listen to the conversations. Circle A, B or C.

Conversation 1
How does Jack feel about the Biology project?
A fed up
B excited
C bored

Conversation 2
How does Ryan see the future of food?
A We'll eat pills.
B We won't eat pasta.
C We'll still eat normal food.

Conversation 3
What does Sue think Sofia should do so that she will feel good again?
A go to the gym
B go dancing
C lie in the sun

2 🔊50 Listen to the conversations again and write (T) true or (F) false.

Conversation 1
1 Jack won't enjoy the project. ☐
2 They will have to work hard. ☐

Conversation 2
3 Ryan doesn't like pasta. ☐
4 Ava thinks robots will cook for them. ☐

Conversation 3
5 Sue is on her way to the park. ☐
6 Sofia likes lying in the sun. ☐

DIALOGUE

1 Complete the conversation. Use the correct phrases to express sympathy.

What a shame | sorry to hear | Poor

ALEX   Hi, Naomi. What seems to be the problem?
NAOMI   It's about Chris, my brother.
ALEX   What about him?
NAOMI   He's in hospital.
ALEX   I'm ¹_____ that, Naomi. What happened?
NAOMI   He broke his leg.
ALEX   ²_____ Chris!
NAOMI   Yes. We wanted to go to the concert on Sunday. Now we can't go.
ALEX   ³_____.

2 Complete the short conversation. Use phrases to express sympathy. Use this situation.

Matthew notices that his friend Owen has a problem. He asks him about it and finds out that Owen lost his wallet on the way to the shopping centre. He lost all his money. He wanted to buy a new MP3 player and can't buy one now.

MATTHEW   Hi, Owen. How are you?
OWEN   _____
          _____
          _____
          _____
          _____
          _____

PHRASES FOR FLUENCY SB p.109

1 Complete the conversation. Replace the phrases in *italics* with phrases from the list.

I suppose so. | I mean | Whatever. | I can't wait.
Wait and see. | Tell you what.

ADRIAN   Looks like it'll start raining pretty soon.
SHEILA   ⁰*I think perhaps you are right.*
ADRIAN   ¹*I really don't care.* I've got so much work to do, so I can't go out anyway.
SHEILA   ²*Here's what I think.* I could help you, then we could go out together. ³*What I want to say is,* if that's OK with you, of course.
GAVIN   ⁴*I'm very excited.* If the weather's OK, we'll climb a mountain on Saturday. It's 3,560 metres high!
ANNE   Wow. That's a lot of walking. Do you think you'll be strong enough?
GAVIN   ⁵*We'll know in the future.*

0   *I suppose so.*
1   _____
2   _____
3   _____
4   _____
5   _____

Reading and Writing part 8

1   Read the information about a doctor's appointment. Complete Dan's notes.

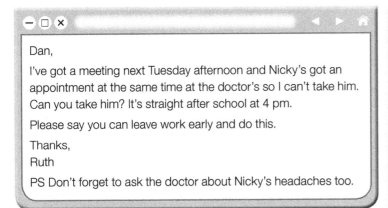

Dan,

I've got a meeting next Tuesday afternoon and Nicky's got an appointment at the same time at the doctor's so I can't take him. Can you take him? It's straight after school at 4 pm.

Please say you can leave work early and do this.

Thanks,
Ruth

PS Don't forget to ask the doctor about Nicky's headaches too.

Garden Lane Medical Centre
14 Garden Lane
Warrington
Phone 01033 325 786

Patient name: Nicholas Holmes

Just to inform you there is a change to your appointment with Dr Glass. The date is now Tuesday 13 October at the same time of 4 pm.

Please let us know if you are unable to make this appointment. Otherwise there is no need to reply. Sorry if this causes you a problem.

Nicky's appointment:

Date: ⁰ *Tuesday 13 October*

Time: ¹ _____

Doctor: ² _____

Address: ³ _____

Phone: ⁴ _____

Don't forget to ask about: ⁵ _____

Exam guide: information transfer

In a form completion question, you will read two short texts and use them to complete some notes about the information they contain.

- You need to read <u>both</u> texts carefully before you try to complete the notes.
- Often information in one text will be different from the information in the other one. This is because the second text often talks about changes. You need to make sure you use the most current information to complete the note.

- Sometimes you will need to work out dates and times using clues in the texts. For example, the first text might say *Let's meet at 10 am* and the second might say *I'll be an hour late*. From these clues the answer for 'time of meeting' will be *11 am*.
- If you have time, always check your answers to see if you missed anything.

2   Read the information about a school trip. Complete Seb's notes.

Dear Seb,

I got the tickets – we're going to see MegaMan! I'm coming up the night before. Can I stay the night at your house? My train arrives at 6 pm. Can you meet me at the station?

Can't wait!
Paul

PS You owe me £25 for the show.

Liverpool Apollo Theatre

Thursday 8 May – One Night Only

MegaMan – Live

Doors open at 7 pm

Paul arrives on: ⁰ *Wednesday 7 May*

Meet him at the station at: ¹ _____

Date of show: ² _____

Name of concert hall: ³ _____

Need to get to the theatre by: ⁴ _____ o'clock.

Ticket costs: ⁵ £_____

12 TRAVELLERS' TALES

GRAMMAR

Present perfect simple `SB p.112`

1 ★☆☆ **Find twelve past participles in the word search. Use the irregular verb list on page 128 to help you.**

R	D	S	L	E	P	T	S	F
T	O	W	S	L	E	E	P	L
A	N	U	V	U	M	S	O	E
K	E	M	S	E	E	N	K	W
E	B	W	R	I	T	T	E	N
N	O	W	R	O	T	E	N	A
A	U	F	L	O	W	N	G	R
S	G	W	A	N	O	R	O	N
T	H	D	G	O	N	E	E	O
O	T	H	E	R	T	A	S	D

0	buy	*bought*	6	sleep	_____
1	do	_____	7	speak	_____
2	fly	_____	8	swim	_____
3	go	_____	9	take	_____
4	meet	_____	10	win	_____
5	see	_____	11	write	_____

2 ★★☆ **Complete the sentences. Use the past participles from Exercise 1.**

0 I have never ___*flown*___ in a plane.

1 My brother has _____ to a lot of football matches this year.

2 I don't want to watch that film – I've _____ it five times!

3 I'm having a great holiday. I've _____ hundreds of photographs!

4 He's really tired because he's _____ fifty emails today.

5 They haven't got any money left because they've _____ so many things.

6 My dad's really happy because he's _____ a competition.

7 The teacher's angry with us because we haven't _____ our homework.

3 ★★☆ **When Jenny was 12, she wrote a list of things she wanted to do. Jenny is now 75. Write sentences about what she has and hasn't done. Use the present perfect form of the verbs.**

0	write a book	✓
1	see the Himalaya mountains	✓
2	fly in a hot air balloon	✗
3	meet the president	✗
4	sleep under the stars	✓
5	swim to France	✗
6	win a tennis tournament	✗
7	go for a walk in the snow – with no shoes!	✓

0 *She's written a book.*

1 _____

2 _____

3 _____

4 _____

5 _____

6 _____

7 _____

been to vs. *gone to* `SB p.112`

4 ★★☆ **Match the pictures and the sentences.**

0 He's been to China. [b]

1 He's gone to China. ☐

2 They've been to the supermarket. ☐

3 They've gone to the supermarket. ☐

Present perfect with *ever* / *never*

SB p.113

5 ★★☆ **Put the words in order to make questions and answers.**

0 A you / ever / a / won / Have / competition
Have you ever won a competition?

B never / I've / No, / anything / won
No, I've never won anything.

1 A been / Has / New York / to / ever / she
_____

B never / the USA / she's / to / been / No,
_____

2 A you / eaten / ever / Have / food / Japanese
_____

B restaurant / been / never / No, / Japanese / I've / to / a
_____

3 A ever / they / in a helicopter / Have / flown
_____

B never / flown / they've / in a helicopter or a plane / No,
_____

4 A your parents / Have / ever / angry with you / been
_____

B they've / angry / with me / lots of times / Yes, / been
_____

Present perfect vs. past simple SB p.115

6 ★★☆ **Complete the conversations. Use the present perfect or past simple form of the verbs in brackets.**

1 A Let's go and eat some Indian food.
B But I ⁰ *'ve never eaten* (never/eat) Indian food.
A No, you're wrong! You ¹_____ (eat) Indian food at my house last week.
B Really? Oh yes – you ²_____ (make) a curry! I remember now.

2 A My parents ³_____ (travel) to lots of places round the world.
B ⁴_____ (they/visit) China?
A Oh, yes, they ⁵_____ (go) to Beijing two years ago. They ⁶_____ (love) it there.
B They're lucky. I ⁷_____ (always/want) to go to China, but I ⁸_____ (never/have) the chance.

Pronunciation

Sentence stress

Go to page 121.

7 ★★★ **Complete the email. Use the present perfect or past simple form of the verbs in brackets.**

Hi Mark,

Sorry I ⁰ *haven't written* (write) to you recently – the thing is, I ¹_____ (be) really busy in June and July!

Anyway, I've got news for you. Two things ²_____ (happen) that are important for me.

So, my first big news is that last week I ³_____ (go) to a party at my friend's house and I ⁴_____ (meet) a really nice girl called Joanna. We ⁵_____ (talk) the whole evening and we ⁶_____ (get) on together really well.

So that's good, eh? Only there's a problem, because at the end of the evening she ⁷_____ (ask) me to go ice-skating with her. Of course I ⁸_____ (say) yes! But I ⁹_____ (never/try) ice-skating before. Should I go? I don't want to look stupid, you know?

The other big news is – my parents ¹⁰_____ (buy) a house! So next month we won't live in this flat any more. I'm a bit sad because I ¹¹_____ (live) here all my life so far, so it's going to be strange to be in another place. But the new house is great – it's got four bedrooms so my brother and I can each have a room. I ¹²_____ (never/have) my own bedroom before! I hope you can come and stay some time.

OK, I have to go now. Write soon OK?

Best, Andy

GET IT RIGHT!
Present perfect with *ever* / *never*

We use *never* when we want to say 'at no time in (my/your/his, etc.) life' and we use *ever* when we want to say 'at any time in (my/your/his, etc.) life'.

✓ I've seen 'War Horse'. It's the best film I've ever seen.

✗ I've seen 'War Horse'. It's the best film I've never seen.

Remember, we don't use *not* and *never* together.

Circle the correct adverb.

1 Lindsay was the best friend I've *never* / *ever* had.

2 I've *never* / *ever* been to London, but I hope to next year.

3 I'm nervous about flying because I've *never* / *ever* done it before.

4 I'm wearing my new shoes. They're the best shoes I've *never* / *ever* had.

5 I have *never* / *ever* visited Paris.

VOCABULARY

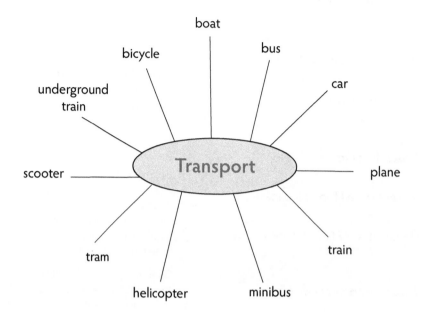

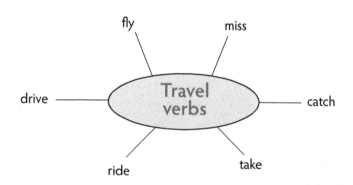

Irregular past participles

been (*go*)	eaten (*eat*)
gone (*go*)	taken (*take*)
done (*do*)	flown (*fly*)
seen (*see*)	swum (*swim*)
written (*write*)	won (*win*)
met (*meet*)	made (*make*)
spoken (*speak*)	driven (*drive*)

Key words in context

continent	The biggest **continent** is Asia.
journey	The **journey** from Japan to France is very long.
neighbour	We have a nice flat but our **neighbours** are terrible – they make a lot of noise!
skeleton	We found some bones on the hill – it was the **skeleton** of a dog.
take a risk	You can't always be safe – sometimes you have to **take a risk**.
tiny	It was a very small mistake – a **tiny** mistake!
tourist	The centre of Paris is always full of **tourists**.
tracks	There was an accident when the train came off the **tracks**.
traveller	Nora Dunn is a professional **traveller**.

Transport and travel `SB p.115`

1 ★☆☆ **Look at the pictures. Use them to complete the puzzle. What is the 'mystery' word?**

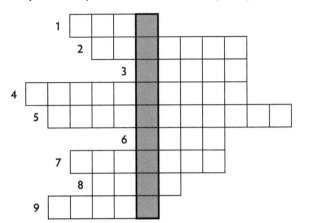

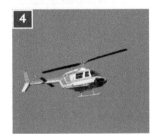

2 ★★☆ **Match the methods of travel and the definitions.**

0 a minibus	*g*
1 (an) underground (train)	
2 a tram	
3 a boat	
4 a plane	
5 a bicycle	
6 a train	
7 a scooter	
8 a helicopter	

a an electric 'train' in cities, for carrying people
b a small motorbike
c something that travels on tracks and carries people
d something that flies and can fly up, down or stay still
e a train that goes below the ground
f something for travelling on water
g a small bus with seats for about ten people
h something with two wheels that you sit on and move with your legs and feet
i something that flies, with engine(s) and wings

Travel verbs `SB p.115`

3 ★☆☆ **Complete the sentences. Use the verbs in the list.**

~~flies~~ | drive | catch | misses | rides | take

0 Aziz is a pilot. He __*flies*__ A380 planes for Emirate Airlines.
1 I don't go by car. I always _____ the train.
2 He hasn't got a car because he can't _____ .
3 She is always at the station ten minutes before her train leaves. She never _____ it.
4 Every weekend he takes his motorbike and _____ it all the way to Scotland.
5 Please don't be late! It's really important that we _____ the 10.30 train.

4 ★★☆ **Complete the sentences. Use the correct form of the travel verbs.**

0 Last year we __*flew*__ from London to Los Angeles.
1 Sometimes I'm late for school because I _____ the bus.
2 My mum _____ to work every day – in her twenty-year old car!
3 On Sunday afternoons, when I'm bored, I go out and _____ my bike for an hour or two.
4 Hurry up! We have to _____ the 10 o'clock train!
5 When we got back to the airport, we _____ a taxi home.

READING

1 REMEMBER AND CHECK (Circle) the correct words. **Check your answers in the blog on page 111 of the Student's Book.**

0 Nora Dunn is a professional (traveller) / tourist.

1 When she was 30, she made a big *mistake* / *decision*.

2 Nora *has* / *hasn't* got rich parents who help her to travel.

3 She has been on TV in *three* / *five* countries.

4 She helped people in Burma and Thailand when *a cyclone* / *an earthquake* hit their countries.

5 Nora writes *in a magazine* / *on a website* to give advice to travellers.

2 Read the story. Answer the questions.

1 What question do the two travellers ask the old man?

_____

2 What two different answers does he give them?

_____

3 Answer the questions.

0 What was the old man looking at when he was on the bench?

He was looking at the town where he lived.

1 What did the first traveller say about the people in the last town he was in?

_____

2 What did the first traveller decide to do – go to the town or not?

_____

3 What were the people like in the last town the second traveller was in?

_____

4 Where did the second traveller go when he left the old man?

_____

4 What does the story tell us? Choose one explanation.

1 If we travel to different places, we will meet all kinds of different people and we can visit them.

2 Whether a place and the people there are nice or not is up to us.

3 Before we visit a place, it's a good idea to ask questions about the people who live there.

One evening, an old man was sitting on a bench on the top of a hill. He was looking down at the town where he lived, down in the valley below him.

Just then, a traveller walked up to him – a man carrying a stick with a small bag on it containing his possessions. He stopped beside the old man to talk to him.

'Excuse me, sir,' the traveller said. 'I am going to the town down there, the town in the valley. Do you know it?'

'Yes,' said the old man. 'I know it.'

'Well,' said the traveller. 'Can you tell me – what are the people like in that town?'

The old man thought for a bit. Then he said, 'Tell me – what were the people like in the last town you were in?'

'Oh,' said the traveller. 'They were awful – horrible people. They didn't like me, and I didn't like them.'

And the old man said, 'I'm sorry to tell you that the people in the town in the valley are horrible too. You won't like them.'

'OK,' said the traveller. And he walked away. He didn't go to the town in the valley.

About an hour later, another traveller arrived near the old man.

'Excuse me, sir,' the second traveller said. 'I am going to the town down there, the town in the valley. Do you know it?'

'Yes,' said the old man. 'I know it.'

'Well,' said the second traveller. 'Can you tell me – what are the people like in that town?'

The old man thought for a bit. Then he said, 'Tell me – what were the people like in the last town you were in?'

'Oh,' said the second traveller. 'They were wonderful – really nice people. They liked me, and I loved them.'

And the old man said, 'I'm happy to tell you that the people in the town in the valley are wonderful too. You are going to like them very much.'

'Oh, thank you!' said the second traveller. And he walked happily down to the town in the valley.

DEVELOPING WRITING

A composition

1 Read the advertisement for a competition in a teenage magazine. Answer the questions.

1 What do you have to write about?

_____

2 How many winners are there?

_____

3 What is the prize for the winners?

_____

HAVE YOU EVER IMAGINED YOUR LIFE IN THE FUTURE? WHEN YOUR DREAMS HAVE COME TRUE?

Write a composition and tell us about you in twenty years' time – where you are and what you've done. (Don't write 'I' – use your name and 'he' or 'she'.)

The winners – there will be three of them! – get a trip to our magazine headquarters in London, to spend a day talking to us and meeting some of the people we write about!

Send your entry to us at:
competition@teenzines.com

CLOSING DATE: 21 DECEMBER

2 Read Jackie's entry composition for the competition. Put the paragraphs in order.

3 It's important in a 'biography' like this to show the times when things happened. Read Jackie's composition again. Complete the phrases that she uses.

0 _From_ 2015 _to_ 2021

1 A year _____ ,

2 _____ she left school

3 at _____ 22

4 After _____ years,

5 _____ 2035,

Writing tip: a composition

This writing task asks you to imagine yourself in the future – and in the future you are doing what you dream of doing. Think about these things.

1 How old is the 'future you'?

2 What are you doing? Where do you live?

3 What happened (e.g. at school) that started you on the road to where you are now?

4 Who helped you?

5 Are you famous? Are you happy?

4 Write your 'story' in the third person, like Jackie did (about 120–160 words). Remember to use time expressions.

From Bradford to Boston!

☐ **A** After a couple of years, her boss asked to see her. 'How about working in the USA?' he said. 'Our owners have a newspaper there. They want you to work for them. In Boston!' Jackie thought for about two seconds and said, 'Yes!'

☐ **B** From 2015 to 2021, Jackie was a student at the Bridges High School in Bradford. She did well at school and enjoyed writing. But her great love was always films – she went to the cinema, she read film magazines, she watched older films on the Internet. Her dream was to work in the USA.

☐ **C** So now, in 2035, she lives and works in Boston. She's been to film festivals all over the world and she's met almost all the great film stars of the 2020s. Her dream has come true!

[1] **D** Jackie Stephenson, from Bradford, England, is the film critic for an American magazine. Here's her story.

☐ **E** So, when her school started an online magazine, it was clear that she was going to write about films! A year later, the local newspaper heard about her and when she left school, they invited her to do a weekly film column.

☐ **F** Jackie enjoyed working for the local newspaper but soon she wanted to do more. So, she started her own film website at the age of 22. But she went on writing for the newspaper too.

LISTENING

1 🔊 52 **Listen to the conversations, A and B. Match the topics with the conversations.**

0	jobs	B
1	being a waiter	☐
2	the important things in your life	☐
3	a house	☐
4	restaurants	☐

2 🔊 52 **Listen again. Complete the sentences.**

A   Gary and Martha

Martha has ⁰ _always lived_ in this house.
Her parents moved from their flat when she
¹ _____ .

Everything important in Martha's life
² _____ in this house.

B   Sue and Uncle Paul

Uncle Paul works in a ³ _____ .
He has also been a ⁴ _____ and a
⁵ _____ .
He hated being a ⁶ _____ but he loved
being a ⁷ _____ .
He has ⁸ _____ a job.

DIALOGUE

1 🔊 52 **Put the conversations in order. Then listen again to check.**

Conversation A

1	GARY	This is a nice house, Martha. Have you always lived here?
☐	GARY	Like what, for example?
☐	GARY	Where have they lived, then?
☐	GARY	Because it's big?
☐	GARY	Oh right. And when you were born, they moved?
☐	MARTHA	Well, a long time ago, they lived in a small flat. Before I was born.
☐	MARTHA	Oh, Gary, I'm not going to tell you!
☐	MARTHA	Yes, we have. Well, I've always lived here, but of course my parents have lived in other places.
☐	MARTHA	Yes, they needed more room. Anyway, I've always loved this house.
☐	MARTHA	No, I don't think it's very big. It's because everything important in my life has happened here.

Conversation B

1	SUE	Uncle Paul? You work in a bank, right?
☐	SUE	A waiter? Really?
☐	SUE	Oh right. And you've been a taxi driver too?
☐	SUE	Have you ever not had a job?
☐	SUE	What other jobs?
☐	SUE	But have you always worked in a bank?
☐	PAUL	No, not always. I've done other jobs too.
☐	PAUL	Yes, that's right.
☐	PAUL	Well, let me think. I've been a waiter and I've been a taxi driver.
☐	PAUL	Yes, I was a waiter when I was at university. Just weekends and holidays. Hard work but good fun! I loved it.
☐	PAUL	No, I've always had a job. I've been very lucky.
☐	PAUL	Yes, I drove a taxi for almost a year. I hated it!

▮▮TRAIN TO THiNK▮▮

Exploring differences

1 **Look at the phrases about jobs in the left-hand column. Are they true about only waiters, about only taxi drivers, or about both? Tick (✓) the correct column.**

You …	waiters	taxi drivers	both
meet a lot of people.			✓
spend a long time on your feet.			
have to carry things.			
can work in any weather.			
have to remember things.			
wear special clothes.			

2 **Think about houses and flats. What things are the same? What things are different? Write three more things in the left-hand column. Tick (✓) the correct column.**

It …	house	flat	both
has got bedrooms.			✓
_____			
_____			
_____			

Reading and Writing part 9

1 Read Georgina's email. Imagine you are Jana. Write an email to Georgina and answer her questions (about 25–35 words).

From: Georgina Morrison

To: Jana Navodna

Hi Jana,

I'm so happy that you can come and stay with us here in Manchester. Is there any food that you really like? Or any food that you really, really don't like?

Is there anywhere in Britain that you really want to go and see?

And (this question's from my brother!) do you want to see any sport while you are here?

Exam guide: guided writing

This exam exercise tests your ability to write a short email / letter / post. You need to:

- Make sure that you do what the task asks you – in other words, write an email (starting, for example, *Hi Georgina*) and answer all three of the questions (in this example, they are about food, places to visit and sport).

- Write the number of words you are asked to write (not fewer than 25, not more than 35).
- Make your English grammar and vocabulary as good as it can be – but the most important thing is to be clear, and to do the points explained above!

2 Read Alex's email. Imagine you are Rodrigo. Write an email to Alex and answer his questions (about 25–35 words).

From: Alex Smith

To: Rodrigo Almeida

Hi Rodrigo,

I was really happy to get your email. I'd like to know something more about you. What kind of films do you really like to watch?

Do you like sport? If you do, which ones?

Who are your best friends?

Write soon!

Alex

CONSOLIDATION

LISTENING

1 🔊 53 **Listen to the conversation. Circle A, B or C.**

1 What happened to Will?
   A He fell off his bike and hurt his shoulder.
   B He fell off his motorbike and hurt his back.
   C He fell off his motorbike and hurt his shoulder.

2 What does Will think is dangerous?
   A driving in traffic
   B riding a bicycle
   C riding a motorbike

3 How does Will usually get to work now?
   A by motorbike
   B by car
   C by bus

2 🔊 53 **Listen again. Answer the questions.**

0 When did Will buy his motorbike?
   He bought it two weeks ago.

1 Why did he buy a motorbike?
   _____

2 Why doesn't he want to use the underground?
   _____

3 When will Will get on his motorbike again?
   _____

4 What does he like about going to work by bus?
   _____

3 Complete the sentences with *been* or *gone*.

TIM   Your dad travels a lot. Where is he this time?

ALICE He's [1] _____ to Brazil.

TIM   Lucky him! Have you ever [2] _____ to Brazil?

ALICE No, I haven't. I've never [3] _____ anywhere outside Europe.

TIM   Where's your sister by the way?

ALICE She's [4] _____ to the dentist's with my mum.

TIM   I haven't [5] _____ to the dentist's for a long time.

GRAMMAR

4 Complete the conversations. Use the present perfect form of the verbs in brackets.

0 A Where's Jack?
   B I don't know. I _*haven't seen*_ (not see) him today.

1 A Are Steve and Julie here?
   B No, they _____ (go) to the cinema.

2 A Is there any food in the kitchen?
   B No – my brother _____ (eat) it all!

3 A _____ (you/write) to your Aunt Paula?
   B Not yet. I'll do it tonight.

4 A Are you enjoying Los Angeles?
   B It's great. I _____ (meet) lots of nice people.

5 A Have you got a lot of homework?
   B No, only a little – and I _____ (do) it all!

6 A Is this a good book?
   B I don't know. I _____ (not read) it.

7 A Why are you so happy?
   B My parents _____ (give) me a new bike for my birthday!

VOCABULARY

5 Complete the words.

0 Can we watch this film? I haven't s *e e n* it before, but everyone says it's great.

1 Some really rich people fly between cities by h _ _ _ _ _ _ _ _ _ _ .

2 He can't walk now because he's broken his a _ _ _ _ .

3 In some European cities you can still see t _ _ _ s that run on metal tracks.

4 He looked really bored, with his e _ _ _ _ _ s on the table and his head between his hands.

5 Wow! It's my first time on a plane! I've never f _ _ _ _ _ before today!

6 We were late, so we didn't c _ _ _ _ the train.

7 The dog was really hot – its t _ _ _ _ _ was hanging out of its mouth.

6 (Circle) the correct words.

JAKE Hi, Mum. I've ⁰(been) / gone into town – and look! I've ¹buy / bought a new shirt.

MUM It's nice, Jake. But isn't it a bit small? You're tall and you've got big ²shoulders / ankles.

JAKE No, Mum, it's fine. I think ³I wear / I'll wear it to Andrea's party on Saturday.

MUM Oh, is she having a party?

JAKE Yes, it's for her birthday. ⁴She's invited / She invites everyone from school.

MUM But her birthday ⁵was / has been last month!

JAKE I know. But her mother was ill, so she couldn't have a party until now.

MUM Oh, I'm sorry to ⁶know / hear that. Is her mother OK now?

JAKE Oh, yes, she's ⁷being / doing OK. She had a problem with her ⁸stomach / knee – the doctors think she ⁹ate / has eaten something bad.

MUM Oh, ¹⁰sorry / poor her. Well, please tell Andrea that I hope the party is great.

JAKE Thanks, Mum. I'll tell her when I ¹¹see / will see her.

DIALOGUE

7 Complete the conversation. Use the words in the list. There are two that you don't need.

been | as soon as | doing | gone | hear | if
knee | poor | shame | went | will | won't

PAUL Hi, Jacky. Where have you ⁰ ___been___ ?

JACKY At the doctor's. I have a pain in my ¹_____ .

PAUL Oh, I'm sorry to ²_____ that. Is everything OK now?

JACKY So-so. I'll have to see him again ³_____ it doesn't get better.

PAUL ⁴_____ you.

JACKY Oh, it's not so bad. It hurts a bit but I'm ⁵_____ OK. Listen, I'm looking for Mike. Do you know where he is?

PAUL Oh, he isn't here. He's ⁶_____ to see his grandmother. She's ill. He ⁷_____ be back until about six o'clock.

JACKY That's a ⁸_____ . I really want to talk to him. Can you ask him to call me, please?

PAUL Sure. I'll ask him ⁹_____ he gets back.

READING

8 Read the text about children and schools in Niger. Answer the questions.

0 In Niger, what percentage of people have running water at home?

20% of people have running water at home.

1 Who often goes to get water for a family?

2 Why is Sani often two hours late for school?

3 Why does Badjeba sometimes fall asleep in lessons?

4 Why do families send children to get water when it makes them late for school?

SCHOOL OR WATER?

Niger, in central Africa, is a country that has very little rain. And 80% of people have no running water at home. So water is very important in people's lives, but sometimes it means that kids don't do well at school.

Children are often the ones who have to find water for the family. They go out on donkeys and travel up to ten kilometres to get water. And then they are late for school, or they don't go at all. Sani, 11, gets water for his family in the morning and usually gets to school at 10 o'clock – two hours late. 'Some of the other children are lucky,' he says. 'They don't have to get water. And so they learn more quickly than me.'

It's hard for the children to study. One girl, Badjeba, says, 'I get up at 4.30 to get water, five kilometres away. Then I take it home. Then I walk to school. I'm exhausted. I'm so tired that I fall asleep in the lessons. And after school, I have to go and find water again.'

In one classroom, the teacher asks: 'How many of you were late today because you had to get water?' And about 90% of the kids put their hand up. Their families send them to get water – school is important, but water is life.

WRITING

9 Imagine you are either Sani or Badjeba (or one of the children in the Culture text on page 116 of the Student's Book). Write a diary entry for a school day (about 100–120 words). Write about these things.

● Getting to school.

● What you did at school.

● Going home.

PRONUNCIATION

UNIT 7
Vowel sounds: /ʊ/ and /uː/

1 🔊32 **What are you buying? Put your finger on** *Start.* **Listen to the words. Go left if you hear the /ʊ/ sound and right if you hear the /uː/ sound. Say the word at the end. You'll hear the words twice.**

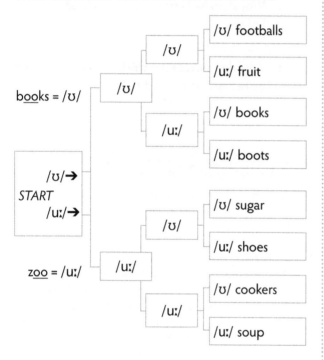

books = /ʊ/

START /ʊ/→ /uː/→

zoo = /uː/

- /ʊ/ footballs
- /uː/ fruit
- /ʊ/ books
- /uː/ boots
- /ʊ/ sugar
- /uː/ shoes
- /ʊ/ cookers
- /uː/ soup

0 book – cool – rule. What do you buy? *boots*

1 _____ 2 _____ 3 _____ 4 _____ 5 _____

2 🔊33 **Listen, check and repeat.**

3 **All of these words are written with the letters 'oo' but they are not pronounced in the same way. Write each word in the /ʊ/ or /uː/ column.**

l̶o̶o̶k̶ | choose | cook | cool
food | good | school | stood

/ʊ/ – foot	/uː/ – room
look	

4 a Which words rhyme with *should*?
_____ **and** _____ .

b Which word rhymes with *shoes*? _____ .

5 🔊34 **Listen, check and repeat.**

UNIT 8
Strong and weak forms of *was* and *were*

1 **Write** *was, wasn't, were* **or** *weren't* **to complete the sentences.**

1 A ___*Was*___ she happy to get her new bike?
  B Yes, she _____. She loves it.
2 A _____ they playing volleyball in the park?
  B No, they _____. They _____ at the beach.
3 A Look – that girl _____ at the pool yesterday.
  B No, she _____!
  A Yes, she _____! She's a good swimmer.
  B She _____. The girl we saw had long brown hair.
4 A They _____ very happy with the restaurant last night.
  B Really? Why not?
  A Because they _____ waiting for their food for a long time.
5 A _____ you at the football match last night?
  B No, I _____. I _____ studying for an exam.
  A _____ you? So was I!

2 🔊35 **Listen, check and repeat.**

3 **Circle the stressed forms of these verbs.**

4 🔊35 **Listen again and check.**

UNIT 9
Vowel sounds: /ɪ/ and /aɪ/

1 **Write the words in the columns.**

g̶i̶v̶e̶ | find | fine | gym | list | nice | night
sing | smile | spring | style | thin | wild | wish

/ɪ/ – think	/aɪ/ – drive
give	

2 🔊40 **Listen, check and repeat.**

3 Match to make sentences.

0 I'm going to keep fit
1 Kim doesn't like
2 Lions and tigers
3 Mike exercises and
4 It's a nice day so let's
a driving at night.

b has a healthy lifestyle.
c ride our bikes.
d classes at the gym.
e are happier in the wild.

4 ◄))41 **Listen and check.**

5 Circle **all of the words in the sentences with the /aɪ/ sound.**

6 ◄))42 **Listen, check and repeat.**

UNIT 10
Voiced /ð/ and unvoiced /θ/ consonants

1 Complete the sentences.

things | clothes | Earth | Maths | months
then | think | third | Thursday | youth

0 There are so many ___things___ to do in Sydney.
1 Let's go shopping. I want to buy some new _____.
2 These three students came first, second and _____ in the race.
3 My father's birthday's on _____.
4 We had dinner and _____ we went to the theatre.
5 I _____ we should go out to a restaurant tonight.
6 We must look after the _____; it's a beautiful planet.
7 There are twelve _____ in a year.
8 We've got a _____ class after the break.
9 A _____ is a young person.

2 ◄))45 **Listen, check and repeat.**

3 Circle **all the words in the sentences with a** *voiced th* **sound.** Underline **all the words with an unvoiced** *th* **sound.**

UNIT 11
The /h/ consonant sound

1 Complete the sentences with the words in the list.

homework | hair | happy | healthy | hear
help | here | hospital | humans | hurt

0 I'll come to your house when I've finished my History __homework__.

1 It's not _____ to eat too many hamburgers.
2 Harry had to go to the _____ in an ambulance.
3 That suitcase looks heavy. Can I _____ you carry it?
4 Helen's got beautiful long black _____.
5 I couldn't _____ the music because the headphones weren't working.
6 I hope you'll be _____ in your new home.
7 In the future _____ won't have as much hair as they do now.
8 Hilary _____ her knee while she was running yesterday.
9 Can you come _____ and help me please?

2 ◄))47 **Listen, check and repeat.**

UNIT 12
Sentence stress

1 Complete the sentences.

scarf | eggs | English | laptop
farmer | island | cooker | taxi

0 I'm wearing a shirt, a skirt, a hat and a __scarf__.
1 An artist, a doctor, a teacher and a _____.
2 We've got Maths, then Art, then History and then _____.
3 We need a desk, a lamp, a sofa and a _____.
4 We caught a plane and then a train and then a bus and then a _____.
5 We put in flour and sugar and then butter and _____.
6 For sale: a digital camera, a pen drive, a microphone and a _____.
7 We saw a lake, a river a jungle and an _____.

2 ◄))51 **Listen, check and repeat.**

3 Underline the stressed words in the lists.

4 ◄))51 **Listen again, check and repeat.**

5 Look at the stressed words in the sentences 0-7. Then read and circle **the correct word to complete the rule.**

We generally stress words like [1]*nouns / articles* that give us information. We don't generally stress words like [2]*nouns / articles*.

GRAMMAR REFERENCE

UNIT 7
should / shouldn't

1 When we want to say that something is a good idea (or is a bad idea), we can use *should* or *shouldn't*.

*I **should study** this weekend.* (I think it's a good idea.)
*They **shouldn't buy** that car.* (I think it's a bad idea.)
***Should we go** out tonight?* (Do you think this is a good idea?)

2 *Should* is a modal verb. We use *should / shouldn't* + base form of the verb, and the form is the same for all subjects. We don't use any form of *do* in the negative.

*I **should try** to study more.*
*I **shouldn't watch** TV tonight.*
*You **should listen to** different music.*
*You **shouldn't listen to** the same things all the time.*

3 Questions are formed with *should* + subject + base form of the verb. Again, we don't use any form of *do* in questions or short answers.

***Should we tell** her?*
*Yes, we **should**. / No, we **shouldn't**.*
***Should I ask** the teacher?*
*Yes, you **should**. / No, you **shouldn't**.*

have to / don't have to

1 We use *have to* to say that it is necessary or very important to do something.

*I'm late, I **have to go** now. We **have to be** at school at 8.30.*

With a third person singular subject (*he, she, it*), we use *has to*.

*Maggie is very ill – she **has to stay** in bed.*
*My dad **has to go to** York tomorrow for a meeting.*

2 We use the negative form *don't / doesn't have to* to say that it isn't necessary or important to do something.

*It's Sunday, so I **don't have to get up early**.*
*She isn't late – she **doesn't have to hurry**.*

3 We form questions with *do* or *does*.

***Do I have to go** to the dentist?*
***Does he have to go** home now?*

4 All forms of *have to* are followed by the base form of the verb.

mustn't vs. don't have to

1 We use *mustn't* to say that it is necessary or very important <u>not</u> to do something.

*You **mustn't be** late.   I **mustn't forget** to phone Jenny.*

2 *Mustn't* has a different meaning from *don't / doesn't have to*.

*You **don't have to tell** your friends.* (= It isn't necessary for you to tell them, but you can if you want to.)
*You **mustn't tell** your friends.* (= Don't tell your friends – it's a secret!)

UNIT 8
Past continuous

1 We use the past continuous to talk about actions in progress at a certain time in the past.

*In 2012, we **were living** in the USA.*
*At 4 o'clock yesterday afternoon, I **was sitting** in a Maths lesson.*
*Last night, theTV was on, but I **wasn't watching it**.*

2 The past continuous is formed with the past simple of *be* + verb + -*ing*.

*I **was reading** a book. I **wasn't enjoying** it.*
*You **were running** very fast! But you **weren't winning**!*
*Jo **was playing** computer games. She **wasn't studying**.*

3 The question is formed with the past simple of *be* + subject + verb + -*ing*. Short answers are formed with *Yes / No* + pronoun + *was / were* or *wasn't / weren't*.

***Was** James **running**? Yes, he **was**. / No, he **wasn't**.*
***Were** your parents **having** lunch?*
*Yes, they **were**. / No, they **weren't**.*
*What **were** you **studying**?   Why **was** she **crying**?*

Past continuous vs. past simple

1 When we talk about the past, we use the past simple for actions that happened at one particular time. We use the past continuous for background actions.

*When Alex **arrived**, I **was having** dinner.*
*He **was running** very fast and he **didn't see** the tree.*
*Sorry, what **did** you **say**? I **wasn't listening**.*

2 We often use *when* with the past simple, and *while* with the past continuous.

*I was reading **when** the phone **rang**.*
***When** my parents **arrived**, we were having a party.*
*I went into the classroom **while** the teacher **was talking**.*
***While** my father **was running**, he fell into a river.*

UNIT 9
Comparative adjectives

1 When we want to compare two things, or two groups of things, we use a comparative form + *than*.

*I'm **older than** my brother.*
*France is **bigger than** Britain.*
*Your computer is **better than** mine.*

2 With short adjectives, we normally add *-er*.

old → older   cheap → cheaper   clever → cleverer

If the adjective ends in *-e*, we only add *-r*.

nice → nicer   safe → safer

If the adjective ends with consonant + *-y*, we change the *-y* to *-i* and add *-er*.

easy → easier   early → earlier   happy → happier

If the adjective ends in a consonant + vowel + consonant, we double the final consonant and add *-er*.

big → bigger   sad → sadder   thin → thinner

3 With longer adjectives (more than two syllables), we don't change the adjective – we put *more* in front of it.

expensive → **more** expensive
difficult → **more** difficult
interesting → **more** interesting

4 Some adjectives are irregular – they have a different comparative form.

good → **better**   bad → **worse**   far → **further**

Superlative adjectives

1 When we compare something with two or more other things, we use a superlative form with *the*.

Steve is **the tallest** boy in our class.
Brazil is **the biggest** country in South America.

2 With short adjectives, we normally add *-est*.

tall → **the tallest**   short → **the shortest**
old → **the oldest**   clean → **the cleanest**

Spelling rules for the *-est* ending are the same as for the *-er* ending in the comparative form.

nice → nicest   happy → the happiest
safe → the safest   big → the biggest
easy → the easiest   thin → the thinnest

3 With longer adjectives (more than two syllables), we don't change the adjective – we put *the most* in front of it.

delicious → **the most** delicious
important → **the most** important
intelligent → **the most** intelligent
This is **the most important** day of my life.
It's **the most expensive** shop in town.

4 Some adjectives are irregular.

good → **the best**   bad → **the worst**   far → **the furthest**
Saturday is **the best** day of the week.
My team is **the worst** team in the world!

can / can't (ability)

1 We use *can / can't* + the base form of the verb to talk about someone's ability to do something. The form of *can / can't* is the same for every person.

My father **can lift** 100 kg.   My brother **can't swim**.
I **can swim** 5 kilometres.   She **can't spell**.
He **can write** in Chinese.
I **can't lift** heavy things.

2 To make questions, we use *Can* + subject + base form of the verb. Short answers are formed with *Yes / No* + pronoun + *can* or *can't*.

Can your sister **swim**?   Yes, she **can**.
Can you **lift** 50 kilos?   No, I **can't**.

UNIT 10
be going to for plans and intentions

1 We use *be going to* to talk about things we intend to do in the future.

I'm **going to visit** my grandfather tomorrow.
My sister's **going to study** German at university.

2 The form is the present simple of *be* + *going to* + base form of the verb.

I'm **going to stay** at home on Sunday. I'm **not going to go** out.
She's **going to look** around the shops. She **isn't going to buy** anything.
Are you **going to watch** the film?
Is he **going to give** us homework tonight?

Short answers are formed using *Yes / No* + pronoun + the correct form of *be* (positive or negative).

Present continuous for future arrangements

We can use the present continuous to talk about arrangements for the future.

We**'re having** a party next weekend. (It's organised.)
I'm **meeting** my friends in the park tomorrow. (I talked to my friends and we agreed to meet.)
Our parents **are going** on holiday in Spain next month. (They have their airline tickets and hotel reservation.)

Adverbs

1 Adverbs usually go with verbs – they describe an action:

We **walked** home **slowly**.   The train **arrived late**.
Drive carefully!

2 A lot of adverbs are formed by adjective + *-ly*.

quiet → quietly   bad → badly   polite → politely

If the adjective ends in *-le*, we drop the *-e* and add *-y*.

terrible → terribly   comfortable → comfortably

If the adjective ends in consonant + *-y*, we change the *-y* to *-i* and add *-ly*.

easy → easily   happy → happily   lucky → luckily

3 Some adverbs are irregular – they don't have an *-ly* ending.

good → **well**   fast → **fast**   hard → **hard**
early → **early**   late → **late**
I played **well** last week.   He worked **hard** all day.
She ran very **fast**.

4 Adverbs usually come immediately after the verb, or, if the verb has an object, after the object.

She **sings well**.   She **plays** the piano **well**.

UNIT 11
will / won't for future predictions

1 We use *will* (*'ll*) and *won't* to make predictions about the future.

*When I'm older, I'**ll travel** round the world. I **won't stay** here!*
*I'm sure you'**ll pass** the test tomorrow. The questions **won't be** very difficult.*
*In the future, people **will take** holidays on Mars. But people **won't live** there.*

2 We use *will / won't* + base form of the verb, and the form is the same for all subjects. We don't use any form of *do* in the negative.

*You'**ll pass** the test.   You **won't pass** the test.*
*He'**ll pass** the test.   He **won't pass** the test.*

3 Questions are formed with *will* + subject + base form of the verb. Again, we don't use any form of *do* in questions or short answers.

*Will Andrea **go** to university?*
*Yes, she **will**. / No, she **won't**.*
*Will your friends **come** to the party?*
*Yes, they **will**. / No, they **won't**.*

First conditional

1 In conditional sentences there are two clauses, an *if* clause and a result clause. We use the first conditional when it is possible or likely that the situation in the *if* clause will happen in the future.

*If I **pass** the test, my parents **will be** happy. (= It's possible that I will pass, but I'm not sure.)*
*If it **doesn't rain**, we'**ll go** for a walk. (= Perhaps it will rain, but I'm not sure.)*

2 The *if* clause is formed with *If* + subject + present simple. The result clause is formed with subject + *will* + base form of the verb. There is a comma after the *if* clause.

*If we **have** time, we'**ll do** some shopping.*
*If you **don't start** your homework soon, you **won't finish** it tonight.*

3 We can change the order of the two clauses. In this case, there is no comma between the clauses.

*We'**ll do** some shopping if we **have** time.*
*You **won't finish** your homework if you **don't start** it tonight.*

Time clauses with when / as soon as

In sentences about the future, we use the present tense after *when* or *as soon as*, and the *will* future in the main clause. (The structure of these sentences is very like the structure of 1st conditional sentences.)

*When I'**m** 18, I'**ll go** to university.*
*I'**ll call** you as soon as I **get** there.*

UNIT 12
Present perfect simple with ever / never

1 We often use the present perfect to talk about things from the beginning of our life until now.

*Sandro **has travelled** to a lot of different countries. (= from when he was born until now)*
*I **haven't met** your parents. (= at any time in my life, from when I was born until now)*

2 When we use the present perfect with this meaning, we often use *ever* (= *at any time in someone's life*) in questions, and *never* (= *not ever*) in sentences. *Ever* comes between the noun or pronoun and the past participle. *Never* comes immediately after *have / has*.

*Have you **ever** eaten Thai food?*
*I've **never** been interested in cooking.*
*Has he **ever** won a prize in a competition?*
*She's **never** tried to learn another language.*

3 The present perfect is formed with the present tense of *have* + past participle of the main verb. For regular verbs, the past participle has the same *-ed* ending as the past simple. Irregular verbs have different past participles.

Regular verbs	Irregular verbs
*We've **stayed** in Athens three times.*	*We've **been** there three times.*
*Have they ever **climbed** a mountain?*	*Have they ever **flown** in a plane?*

See page 128 for the past participles of irregular verbs.

4 There is a difference between *been* and *gone*.

*I've **been** to the supermarket = I went to the supermarket and now <u>I am back again</u>.*
*They've **gone** to the supermarket = they went to the supermarket and <u>they are still there</u>.*

Present perfect vs. past simple

Both the **present perfect** and the **past simple** refer to the past. But we use the **past simple** to talk about situations or actions at a particular time in the past, and we use the **present perfect** to talk about situations or actions in the past, at an unspecified time between the past and now.

Past simple
*I **ate** sushi **two weeks ago**.*
*I **read** a Shakespeare play **last month**.*
*He **was** late for school **yesterday**.*
*We **didn't buy** anything in town **on Saturday**.*

Present perfect
*I'**ve eaten** sushi a lot of times.*
*I'**ve read** six Shakespeare plays.*
*He'**s been** late to school four times.*
*We **haven't bought** anything in town for a long time.*

IRREGULAR VERBS

Base form	Past simple	Past participle
be	was / were	been
become	became	become
begin	began	begun
break	broke	broken
bring	brought	brought
build	built	built
buy	bought	bought
can	could	-
catch	caught	caught
choose	chose	chosen
come	came	come
cost	cost	cost
cut	cut	cut
do	did	done
draw	drew	drawn
drink	drank	drunk
drive	drove	driven
eat	ate	eaten
fall	fell	fallen
feel	felt	felt
find	found	found
fly	flew	flown
forget	forgot	forgotten
get	got	got
give	gave	given
go	went	gone
grow	grew	grown
have	had	had
hear	heard	heard
hit	hit	hit
keep	kept	kept
know	knew	known
leave	left	left

Base form	Past simple	Past participle
lend	lent	lent
lie	lay	lain
lose	lost	lost
make	made	made
mean	meant	meant
meet	met	met
pay	paid	paid
put	put	put
read /riːd/	read /red/	read /red/
ride	rode	ridden
run	ran	run
say	said	said
see	saw	seen
sell	sold	sold
send	sent	sent
show	showed	shown
sing	sang	sung
sit	sat	sat
sleep	slept	slept
speak	spoke	spoken
spend	spent	spent
stand	stood	stood
swim	swam	swum
take	took	taken
teach	taught	taught
tell	told	told
think	thought	thought
throw	threw	thrown
understand	understood	understood
wake	woke	woken
wear	wore	worn
win	won	won
write	wrote	written

Acknowledgements

The authors and publishers acknowledge the following sources of copyright material and are grateful for the permissions granted. While every effort has been made, it has not always been possible to identify the sources of all the material used, or to trace all copyright holders. If any omissions are brought to our notice, we will be happy to include the appropriate acknowledgements on reprinting.

Emily Cummins for the text on p. 68 adapted from http://www.emilycummins.co.uk/about. Copyright © Emily Cummins. Reproduced with permission.

Corpus
Development of this publication has made use of the Cambridge English Corpus (CEC). The CEC is a computer database of contemporary spoken and written English, which currently stands at over one billion words. It includes British English, American English and other varieties of English. It also includes the Cambridge Learner Corpus, developed in collaboration with Cambridge English Language Assessment. Cambridge University Press has built up the CEC to provide evidence about language use that helps to produce better language teaching materials.

English Profile
This product is informed by the English Vocabulary Profile, built as part of English Profile, a collaborative programme designed to enhance the learning, teaching and assessment of English worldwide. Its main funding partners are Cambridge University Press and Cambridge English Language Assessment and its aim is to create a 'profile' for English linked to the Common European Framework of Reference for Languages (CEF). English Profile outcomes, such as the English Vocabulary Profile, will provide detailed information about the language that learners can be expected to demonstrate at each CEF level, offering a clear benchmark for learners' proficiency. For more information, please visit
www.englishprofile.org

Cambridge Dictionaries
Cambridge dictionaries are the world's most widely used dictionaries for learners of English. The dictionaries are available in print and online at dictionary.cambridge.org. Copyright © Cambridge University Press, reproduced with permission.

The publishers are grateful to the following for permission to reproduce copyright photographs and material:

T = Top, B = Below, L = Left, R = Right, C = Centre, B/G = Background

p.68 (TL): ©REX/Ray Tang; p.68 (TR): ©Emily Cummins http://www.emilycummins.co.uk; p.68 (B): ©Emily Cummins http://www.emilycummins.co.uk; p.69 (TL): ©BrAt82/Shutterstock; p.69 (TR): ©BuddyFly/iStock/360/Getty Images; p.69 (CL): ©REX/Roger Viollet; p.69 (CR): ©George Timakov/Hemera/360/Getty Images; p.69 (B): ©akajhoe/iStock/360/Getty Images; p.75 (snowboard): ©YanLev/Shutterstock; p.75 (golf): ©anek_s/iStock/360/Getty Images; p.75 (windsurf): ©jan kranendonk/iStock/360/Getty Images; p.75 (volleyball): ©Eastimages/Shutterstock; p.75 (skis and poles): ©gorillaimages/Shutterstock; p.75 (football): ©stockphoto-graf/Shutterstock; p.75 (diving board): ©sirastock/Shutterstock; p.75 (helmet and rope): ©grafvision/Shutterstock; p.75 (parallel bars): ©versh/Shutterstock; p.75 (sailing): ©Michael Blann/Photodisc/Getty Images; p.75 (starting block): ©Ulrich Mueller/Shutterstock; p.75 (rugby): ©Paolo De santis/Hemera/360/Getty Images; p.75 (tennis): ©miflippo/iStock/360/Getty Images; p.76 (TR): ©technotr/E+/Getty Images; p.76 (TL): ©Keystone/Hulton Archive/Getty Images; p.76 (BR): ©YTopFoto; p.76 (BL): ©Tony Duffy/Getty Images Sport/Getty Images; p.77: ©Galina Burtseva/iStock/360/Getty Images; p.78 (TL): ©Echo/Cultura/Getty Images; p.78 (TC): ©The Washington Post/Getty Images; p.78 (TR): ©Konstantin Shishkin/iStock/360/Getty Images; p.78 (CL): ©LuckyBusiness/iStock/360/Getty Images; p.78 (C): ©Kzenon/Shutterstock; p.78 (CR): ©Greg Epperson/iStock/360/Getty Images; p.78 (BL): ©Ingram Publishing/Getty Images; p.78 (BC): ©saintho/iStock/360/Getty Images; p.78 (BR): ©Jupiterimages/Stockbyte/Getty Images; p.79: ©Athol Pictures/Alamy; p.81: ©JUNG YEON-JE /AFP/Getty Images; p.86: ©Yvette Cardozo/Photolibrary/Getty Images; p.87: ©Barry Mason/Alamy; p.92 (zebra crossing): ©Stephen Rees/Shutterstock; p.92 (youth club): ©Jeff Morgan 16/Alamy; p.92 (speed camera): ©Howard_M/iStock/360/Getty Images; p.92 (graffiti): ©A_Lesik/Shutterstock; p.92 (cycle lane): ©Aleramo/iStock/360/Getty Images; p.92 (litter bin): ©sunsetman/Shutterstock; p.92 (billboard): ©Jeff Morgan 09/Alamy; p.92 (high street): ©Ingram Publishing/Getty Images; p.92 (skate park): ©moodboard/360/getty Images; p.94 (TL): ©RICK WILKING/Reuters/Corbis; p.94 (TR): ©Claver Carroll/Photolibrary/Getty Images; p.94 (C): ©ArtPix/Alamy; p.94 (B): ©Gideon Mendel/Corbis; p.95: ©David Hughes/Hemera/360/Getty Images; p.99: ©OlgaCanals/iStock/360/Getty Images; p.102 (BL): ©vadimmmus/iStock/360/Getty Images; p.102 (TL): ©Holger Scheibe/Corbis; p.102 (stomachache): ©Shutterstock/Photographee.eu; p.102 (earache): ©Shutterstock/Dora Zett; p.102 (headache): ©ATIC12/iStock/360/Getty Images; p.102 (toothache): ©Thomas Lammeyer/Herma/360/Getty Images; p.104 (L): ©Eric Fleming Photography/Shutterstock; p.104 (R): ©Rich Carey/Shutterstock; p.111 (1): ©JackF/iStock/360/Getty Images; p.111 (2): ©Onoky/Superstock; p.111 (3): ©Kimberly Brotherman/Moment Open/Getty Images; p.111 (4): ©KatPaws/iStock/360/Getty Images; p.111 (5): ©Matthew Grant/iStock/360/Getty Images; p.111 (6): ©Marin Tomas/iStock/360/Getty Images; p.111 (7): ©Charles O. Cecil/Alamy; p.111 (8): ©Shutterstock/Dudarev Mikhail; p.111 (9): ©hxdyl/iStock/360/Getty Images.

Cover photographs by: ©Yuliya Koldovska/Shutterstock; ©Lukasz Pajor/Shutterstock; ©William Perugini/Shutterstock.

The publishers are grateful to the following illustrators:
David Semple 67, 73, 88, 101, 108; Fred Van Deelen (The Organisation) 64, 93; Julian Mosedale 70, 82, 91, 103, 112

The publishers are grateful to the following contributors:
Blooberry Design Ltd: text design and layouts; Claire Parson: cover design; Hilary Fletcher: picture research; Leon Chambers: audio recordings; Karen Elliott: Pronunciation sections; Diane Nicholls: Get it right! exercises